1 MONTH OF
FREE
READING

at

www.ForgottenBooks.com

By purchasing this book you are eligible for one month membership to ForgottenBooks.com, giving you unlimited access to our entire collection of over 1,000,000 titles via our web site and mobile apps.

To claim your free month visit:

www.forgottenbooks.com/free309968

ISBN 978-0-265-44726-0
PIBN 10309968

DANTE

ILLUSTRATIONS

AND NOTES

EDINBURGH

PRIVATELY PRINTED

T. & A. CONSTABLE

1890

PREFACE

*N sending out to his classes this little volume of Notes and Illustrations, Dr. Whyte wishes them to know how much they are indebted to the original and sympathetic* genius *of Mrs. Traquair, to the ripe and various scholarship of the Rev. John Sutherland Black, as well as to the fine taste and professional skill of Mr. Walter Blaikie, of the eminent house to which the production of this book was intrusted.*

ST. GEORGE'S FREE CHURCH,
EDINBURGH, *November*, 1890.

THE CONTENTS

ILLUSTRATIONS

BY PHOEBE ANNA TRAQUAIR

CONTENTS

NOTES

By John Sutherland Black

INFERNO

FIRST AND SECOND

CIRCLES

II

INFERNO

THIRD, FOURTH, FIFTH, AND SIXTH CIRCLES

THIRD, FOURTH, FIFTH, AND SIXTH CIRCLES

The Gluttonous guarded by Cerberus.

The Avaricious and Prodigal guarded by Plutus.

The Wrathful and Melancholy in the Stygian
Pool.

The Heretics in the City of Dis.

INF. vi–xi.

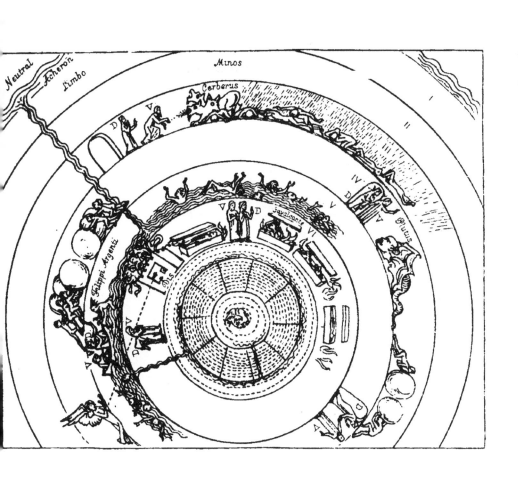

III

INFERNO

THE SEVENTH

CIRCLE

SEVENTH CIRCLE IN THREE SECTIONS

(1) The Violent against Others.
(2) The Violent against Themselves.
(3) The Violent against God, Nature, and Art.

INF. xii-xvii.

xxii

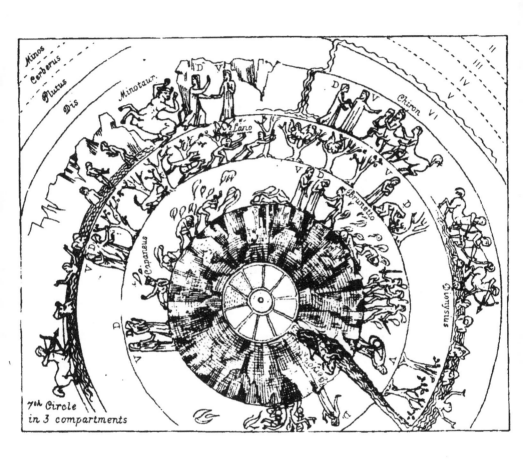

Minos
Cerberus
Plutus
Dis
Minotaur
II
III
IV
V
Chiron VI
D V
D V
D V
Lano
V D
V D
V D
Brunetto
Capareus
A D e
A
D
A
A
Corysus
A D
7th Circle
in 3 compartments

IV

INFERNO

THE EIGHTH

CIRCLE

THE EIGHTH CIRCLE

Descent on Geryon into Malebolge.
The Ten Moats of the Fraüdulent.

INF. xviii–xxx.

xxvi

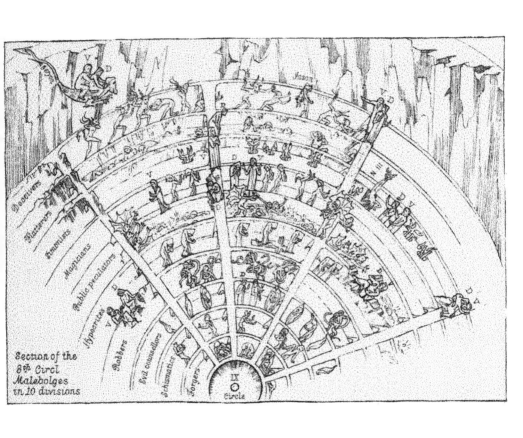

Deceivers

Flatterers

Seducers

Magicians

Public peculators

Hypocrites

Robbers

Evil counsellors

Schismatics

Forgers

Section of the
8th Circl
Malebolges
in 10 divisions

IX
O
Circle

V

INFERNO

THE NINTH CIRCLE

NINTH CIRCLE : COCYTUS

The Well of the Giants.
The Freezing Winds.

INF. xxxi–xxxiv.

VI

PURGATORIO

THE FOOT OF THE
HILL

THE ANTE-PURGATORY

Virgil and Dante emerge at the foot of the Hill
of Purgatory, meet Cato, and see the approach
of the Angel-Pilot.

PURG. i–ii. 44.

VII

PURGATORIO

THE ANTE-PURGATORY

THE ANTE-PURGATORY

Casella, Belacqua, and Sordello

PURG. ii.

xxxviii

VIII

PURGATORIO

THE GATE OF
PURGATORY

THE GATE OF PURGATORY

The Valley of the Princes.
The Gate of Purgatory and the Cornice
    of the Proud.

PURG. vii–xii. 80.

First round in Purgatory Pride punished

Gate of Purgatory

Lucia

Sordello

First night in Purgatory

IX

PURGATORIO

SECOND AND THIRD CORNICES

SECOND AND THIRD CORNICES

The Envious.

The Angry.

PURG. xii. 81–xvii. 63.

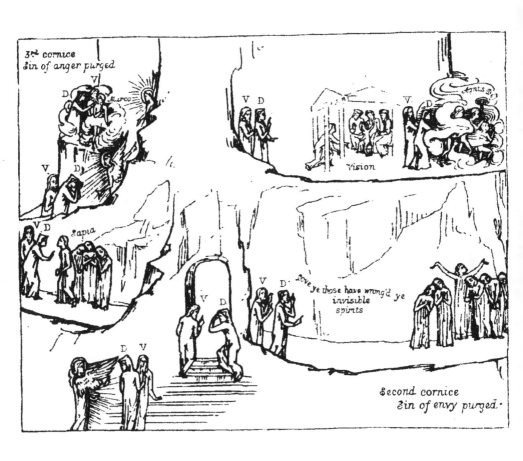

X

PURGATORIO

FOURTH AND FIFTH
CORNICES

FOURTH AND FIFTH CORNICES

The Gloomy and Indifferent.
The Avaricious.

PURG. xvii. 63-xxi.

Pope Ardian V · V D · Status D V · V · D · V S · 5th cornice Sin of avarice cleansed

V · D

Alberto D V · V

Fourth cornice Sin of gloominess or indifference purged · D · 2nd Night & 3rd Morning

XI
PURGATORIO
SIXTH AND SEVENTH
CORNICES

SIXTH AND SEVENTH CORNICES

The Gluttonous.
The Impure.

PURG. xxii–xxvii. 66.

liv

7th Cornice
Sin of incontinence purged.

6th Cornice
Sin of gluttony purged.

XII

PURGATORIO

THE EARTHLY

PARADISE

THE EARTHLY PARADISE

Matilda and the Waters of Lethe.

PURG. xxvii. 67–xxviii.

3rd Night.

Earthly Paradise.

XIII

P U R G A T O R I O

THE WATERS OF

LETHE

THE WATERS OF LETHE

The Vision of the Church Militant.
Beatrice appears.

PURG. xxix-xxxi.

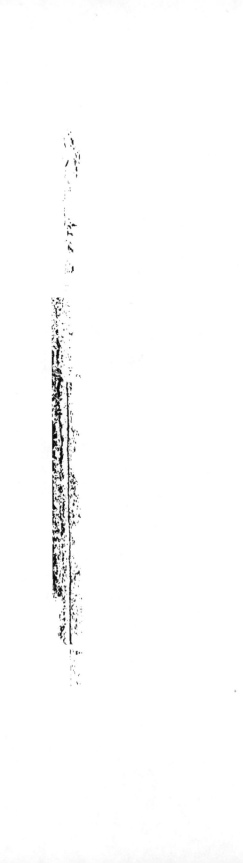

XIV

PURGATORIO

THE WATERS OF
ÉUNOE

THE WATERS OF RUMOR

Vision of the Church and Empire.
xxxii–xxxiii.

lxvi

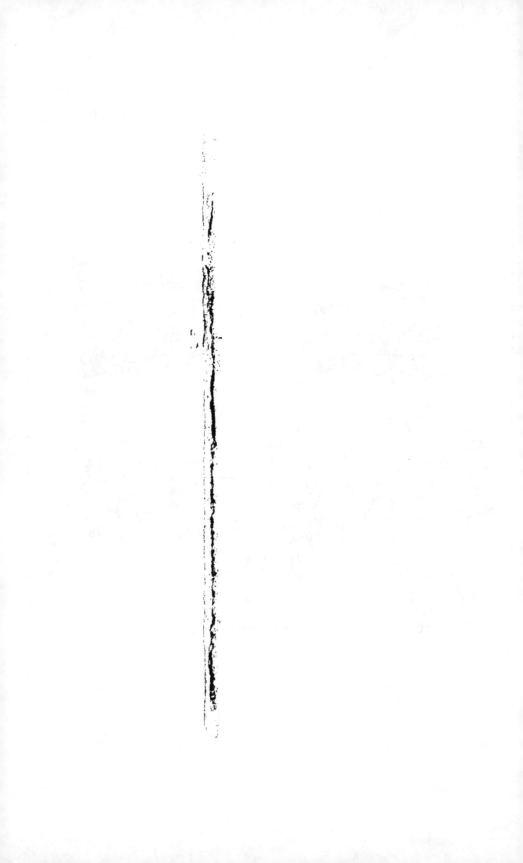

XV

PARADISO

FIRST HEAVEN

Sphere of the Moon, containing
were broken.   ₄

ı

B D ... Mercury

Piccarda

B D

The Moon

B D

1st Heaven

Earthly Paradise

XVI

PARADISO

SECOND AND THIRD

HEAVENS

SECOND AND THIRD HEAVENS

Sphere of Mercury : the Active and Ambitious.
Sphere of Venus : Lovers.

PAR. v. 92–ix.

XVII

PARADISO

FOURTH AND FIFTH

HEAVENS

FOURTH AND FIFTH HEAVENS

Sphere of the Sun : the Wise.
Wreath of Saints and Philosophers.
Sphere of Mars : the Militant.
Martyrs, Confessors, and Warriors.

PAR. x–xviii. 47.

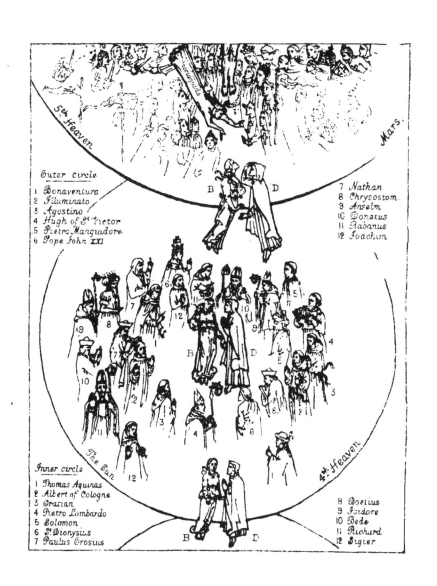

5th Heaven

Mars.

Outer circle

1 Bonaventura
2 Illuminato
3 Agostino
4 Hugh of St Victor
5 Pietro Mangiadore
6 Pope John XXI

7 Nathan
8 Chrysostom
9 Anselm
10 Donatus
11 Rabanus
12 Joachim

The Sun

4th Heaven

Inner circle

1 Thomas Aquinas
2 Albert of Cologne
3 Gratian
4 Pietro Lombardo
5 Solomon
6 St Dionysius
7 Paulus Orosius

8 Boetius
9 Isidore
10 Bede
11 Richard
12 Sigier

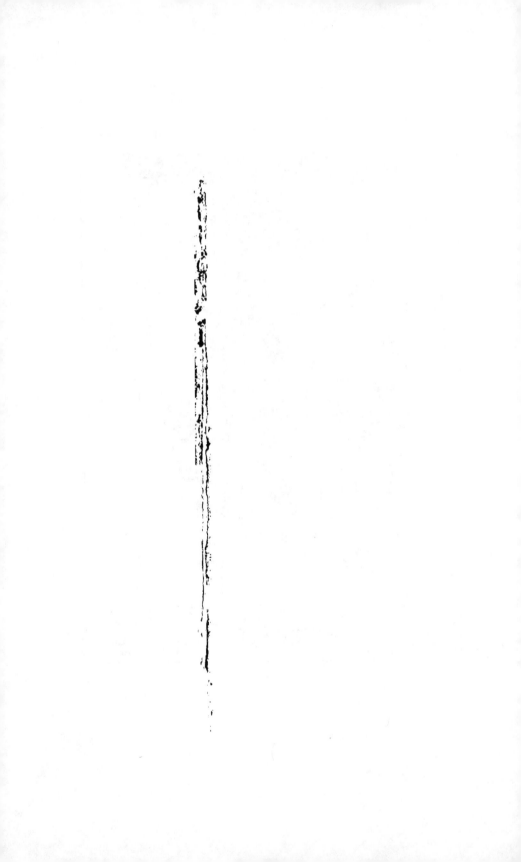

XVIII

PARADISO

SIXTH AND SEVENTH

HEAVENS

SIXTH AND SEVENTH HEAVENS

Sphere of Jupiter : Just Rulers.
The heavenly Eagle.
Sphere of Saturn : The Contemplative.
The holy Ladder.

PAR. xviii. 48–xxii. 101.

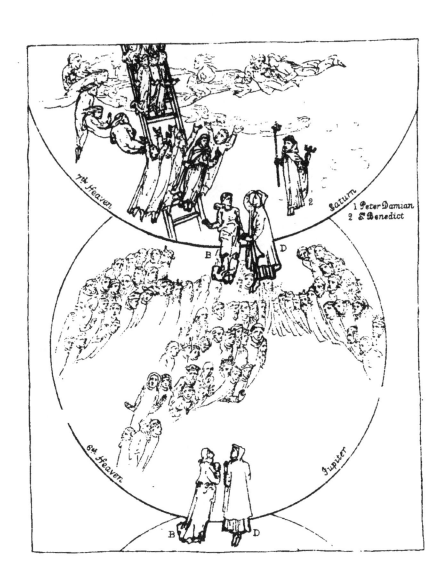

XIX

PARADISO

EIGHTH HEAVEN

EIGHTH HEAVEN

Sphere of the Fixed Stars.
Triumph of Christ and His Church.

PAR. xxii. 102–xxiii.

XX

PARADISO

THE EMPYREAN

THE EMPYREAN

The Nine Dominions and
                    Nine Heavens.
                         PAR. xxiv–xxxiii.

XC

A SCHEME

OF THE

PURGATORY

PROPER

CHASTISEMENT.

1. The Proud.
Cantos x.–xii.

They creep beneath heavy masses of stone (x. 118-139).

2. The Envious.
xiiL–xv. 40.

They sit clothed in sackcloth, and with eyelids sewed up with wire (xiii. 58-72).

3. The Angry.
xv. 82–xvii. 69.

They are surrounded by cloud of smoke-fog (xvi. 1-9 and xvii. 1-9).

4. The Slothful.
xvii. 70–xix. 51.

They run with extreme speed (xviii. 88-98).

5. The Avaricious.
xix. 70–xxi.

They lie prone on the earth (xix. 72).

6. The Gluttonous.
xxii.–xxiv.

They are famished in the midst of plenty (xxii. 130-135; xxiii. 22-39; xxiv. 100-111).

7. The Impure.
xxv. 109–xxvii. 66.

They walk in a furnace (xxv. 112-114).

xciv

PURGATORY-PROPER

MEDITATION.	PRAYER.	BEATITUDE.
Sculptures of humility on the rock wall (x. 31-96) and of pride on pavement (xii. 14-64).	The Lord's Prayer (xi. 1-24).	Blessed are the poor in spirit (xii. 104).
Voices repeat words of the loving and of the envious (xiii. 25-36).	They entreat the prayers of all saints (xiii. 50).	Blessed are the merciful (xv. 38).
Mental visions of meekness (xv. 85-114) and of anger (xvii. 13-39).	O Lamb of God, grant us thy peace (xvi. 16-19).	Blessed are the peacemakers (xvii. 68).
They themselves shout examples of diligence (xviii. 97-105) and of sloth (xviii. 131-138).		Blessed are they that mourn (xix. 50).
By day they praise the poor and the liberal (xx. 17-27), and by night denounce the avaricious (xx. 97-123).	My soul cleaveth unto the dust : quicken thou me (xix. 73).	Blessed are they that thirst after righteousness (xxii. 5).
Examples of temperance (xxii. 140-154) and of gluttony (xxiv. 118-129) are cried out by voices from the trees.	O Lord, open thou my lips (xxiii. 11).	Blessed who only hunger in just measure (xxiv. 151).
They proclaim examples of chastity (xxv. 127-135) and cry shame on instances of impurity (xxvi. 40-48).	' Father of mercies infinite ' (xxv. 121).	Blessed are the pure in heart (xxvii. 8).

A CHRONOLOGY OF
the Life of
DANTE
with mention of some of the
MORE IMPORTANT HISTORICAL EVENTS
which happened within the years of
his earthly journey (1265-1321)
· ESPECIALLY
of those which he has himself
alluded to in his
COMMEDIA

EPRESENTATIVES from boroughs JANUARY first take seats along with prelates, **1265** barons, and knights of the shire, in the national council, or parliament, of England.

FEB. 5. Clement IV. becomes pope. (He is mentioned in *Purg.* iii. 125. See under 1266 and 1268.)

MAY. Birth of Durante (Dante), son of Aldighiero degli Aldighieri, a Florentine lawyer, and of his (second) wife, 'Bella'.

Dante himself tells us (*Par.* xxii. 115-7) that he was born when the sun was in Gemini—not earlier therefore than May 18th, or later than June 17th, in that year. There is some reason for conjecturing that it may have been on the day of a local saint named Lucy (Lucia Ubaldini, sister of the Florentine Cardinal Ottaviano degli Ubaldini referred to in *Inf.* x. 120), *i.e.* on 30th May (see Witte, *D. F.* ii. 29-31). He was baptized in the baptistery (*Par.* xxv. 8). For his ancestry, which he traced back to a crusading knight, Cacciaguida by name (*c.* 1106-*c.* 1148), and through him to an ancient Roman stock, see *Par.* xv. and xvi. The allusion in *Par.* xv. 91 to his grandfather seems to show that he did not know—perhaps did not even care to know—much about him; he aces him vaguely amongst those who are being cleansed from the sin of pride.

MAY–JUNE. Charles of Anjou, brother of Louis IX. of France, lands at Ostia from Marseilles (*Purg.* xx. 67), and on the 23d of May enters Rome. He is made senator of Rome on 21st June, and on 28th June swears homage to the Pope for the kingdom of (Naples and) Sicily.

It was the arrival of the French troops, under Guy de Montfort, in Lombardy in this year that gave Buoso da Duera of Cremona opportunity for the act of treachery against the Ghibelline cause alluded to in *Inf.* xxxii. 115; he allowed the enemy to pass the river unopposed.

AUG. 4. Defeat and death of Simon de Montfort in battle of Evesham.

Duns Scotus, the famous schoolman ('the Subtle Doctor'), was born in Scotland about this time. Though one of the most prominent and distinguished men of his time, he is nowhere alluded to by Dante, nor can his influence be traced in any of the poet's writings.

1266 FEB. The passage of the Garigliano at Ceperano near the Neapolitan frontier is betrayed to the French by Richard, Count of Caserta, Manfred's brother-in-law.

The allusion to Ceperano in *Inf.* xxviii. 16 may perhaps be due to a temporary lapse of memory, and reference be really intended to the battle of Benevento.

FEB. 26. Defeat and death of Manfred, king of Sicily, in battle of Benevento (or of Grandella, as it is sometimes called); see *Purg.* iii. 103-145.

His body, as that of an excommunicate person, found a temporary resting-place under a cairn at the foot of the bridge over the Calore at

2

Benevento, but afterwards at the demand of Bartolommeo Pignatelli, archbishop of Cosenza, instigated by the pope (Clement IV.), who regarded the whole kingdom as consecrated ground, it was disinterred and buried (presumably within flood-mark) on the banks of the Verde (Garigliano), where it separates the Sicilian Kingdom from the States of the Church (*Purg.* iii. 131).

This disaster to the Ghibelline cause drove the Ghibellines in Florence from power, and cleared the way for the 'second' return of the Guelphs alluded to by Dante in his talk with Farinata Degli Uberti (*Inf.* x. 50). (The 'first' return had been in 1250.) It was now that Gianni del Soldanier, a leading Ghibelline, tempted by desire for power, treacherously went over to the Guelphs (*Inf.* xxxii. 121).

APRIL. Birth of her ' who was called Beatrice [*Beatrix*, she who ma e happy] by many who knew not wherefore' (*V. N.* 1). k s

SEP. 29. Niccola Pisano is commissioned to execute his great pulpit in the cathedral of Siena, and to avail himself of the assistance of Arnolfo [di Cambio], Lapo, and his own son Giovanni (Vasari i. 283, 304).

Roger Bacon sends three books of his *Opus Majus* (' the encyclopædia of the 13th century') to Clement IV.

Birth of Giotto (not, as often said, in 1276. See Vasari, *c.* 1266 i. 370).

Charles of Anjou (now Charles I. of Sicily) enters 1267 Florence, and puts himself at the head of the Guelphs, being elected podestà for ten years.

The Ghibellines are permitted to return, but the Uberti are excluded from the general amnesty—whence the question of Farinata, *Inf.* x. 83.

AUG. 26. Conradin, the last of the house of Hohen- 1268 staufen, is defeated by Charles of Anjou at Tagliacozzo, *Inf.* xxviii. 16. (Alardo [di Valleri] was one of Charles's generals. The reference is to a skilful piece of strategy.)

OCT. 29. Execution of Conradin and his cousin, Frederick of Austria, at Naples (*Purg.* xx. 68).

With this event may be said to have terminated an important ' Epoch of Church History,' on which see Count Ugo Balzani's useful little manual, *The Popes and the Hohenstaufen* (1889).

NOV. 29. Death of Pope Clement IV. at Viterbo.

He is mentioned nowhere in the *Commedia* except in *Purg.* iii. 125 (see above), but Dante's estimate of him may fairly enough be held to be implied in *Inf.* xix. 74, where Nicholas III. (see below, under 1280), speaks of his ' predecessors, stained in Simon's sin '.

Niccola Pisano finishes his Siena pulpit. About this year died Vincent of Beauvais, compiler of the *Majus Speculum*, a great and once famous compendium of the knowledge of its time, of which Dante is believed to have made some use.

1269 JUNE 11. Victory of the Florentines (Guelph) over the Sienese (Ghibelline) at Colle di Valdelsa near Volterra, and death of Provenzano Salvani at their head (*Purg.* xi. 109 *sqq.*).

'Of him . . . . all Tuscany used to resound, and now hardly do they whisper of him in Siena, whereof he was lord when the Florentine rage was destroyed' [at Montaperti in 1260]. This victory at Colle is also alluded to in Sapia's story (*Purg.* xiii. 115 *sqq.*).

1270 AUG. 25. Death of Louis IX. (St. Louis) of France in his quarters on the castle hill of ancient Carthage, while besieging Tunis.

Dante's only allusion to this saint is in *Purg.* xx. 61, where it is implied that the double marriage of Louis and his brother Charles, to the two daughters of Raymond Berenger, Count of Provence, was not for the public good. [It had helped to bring about the fall of the Hohenstaufen.] Compare *Purg.* vii. 128. See Giotto's portrait of St. Louis— 'gentle, resolute, glacial, pure'—in the Bardi Chapel, Santa Croce, Florence.

c. 1270 Birth of William of Occam (in Surrey), the ' Invincible Doctor' and ' Venerable Inceptor'. A great schoolman, and a Franciscan, but nowhere alluded to by Dante.

c. 1270 Birth of Cino da Pistoia (Guittoncino de' Sinibaldi), poet, friend of Dante.

1271 MAR. Murder of Henry, son of Richard of Cornwall, and nephew of Henry III., by Guy de Montfort at Viterbo, in revenge for the death of his father Simon (*Inf.* xii. 119).

A DANTE CHRONOLOGY

SEP. 1. Gregory X. (Tebaldo Visconti, archdeacon of Liége), while absent at Acre on church business, is elected successor to Clement IV., at Viterbo.

NOV. Marco Polo of Venice sets out from Acre with his uncles Marco and Maffeo for the court of Kublai Khan.

The elder men had been long detained at Acre, the vacancy in the Papal See preventing them until now from executing the commission laid on them by the Khan.

NOV. 16. Death of Henry III. of England: 'Henry of **1272** simple life' (*Purg.* vii. 131). Edward I. succeeds: 'Henry . . . happier in his branches than most' (*Purg.* vii. 131-2. See below, under 1307).

OCT. 1. Rudolph of Hapsburg is elected emperor (*Purg.* **1273** vii. 94. See below, under 1291).

Gregory X., on his way to Lyons for the meeting of the General Council, visits Florence, and there meets Charles of Anjou (I. of Sicily) and Charles's father-in-law, Baldwin II., ex-emperor of Constantinople. He makes the Guelphs and Ghibellines swear to a treaty of peace and a general amnesty. Shortly after his departure the bond is · broken ; he lays the city under an interdict which continues till 1276.

MARCH 7. Death of Thomas Aquinas (the 'Angelical **1274** Doctor ') at Fossa Nova in Campania, while on his way to the council of Lyons.

Dante (*Purg.* xx. 69) seems to have believed the story (not now credited) that Thomas had been poisoned at the instance of King Charles.

MAY. Dante first sees ' the glorious Lady of his mind '.

It is hardly to be supposed that he noted the event with minute care in his diary at the time, but, looking back on it many years afterwards, he saw that the vision had been the greatest crisis his mental, moral and spiritual history had known. 'Love took up the harp of life.' His heart had said once for all to itself :—' Here is a divinity stronger than I, who, coming, shall rule over me '; his intellect to his eyes :— 'Your beatitude hath now appeared'; the sensuous nature within him :—' Woe is me ! for that often henceforth shall I be hindered.' *V. N.* 2.

' I say that from that time forward love quite governed my soul, which was immediately espoused to him with so safe and undisputed a lord-

5

ship, *by virtue of strong imagination*, that I had nothing left for it but to do all his bidding continually. . . . . Her image was with me always' (*V. N.* 2).

Nor without cause. 'She went along crowned and clothed with humility . . . so gentle and so full of all perfection that she bred in those who looked upon her a soothing quiet beyond any speech . . . and when she had gone by it was said by many, " This is not a woman, but one of the beautiful angels of heaven" : and there were some that said " This surely is a miracle : blessed be the Lord who hath power to work thus marvellously" (*V. N.* 26). Hence 'that reverence, which has the mastery of me wholly, even for the letters of her name' (*Par.* vii. 13).

JUNE 24. Fourteenth general council (second of Lyons) meets at Lyons.

JULY 14. Death of Bonaventura (the 'Seraphic Doctor') at Lyons. (See *Par.* xii. 127-9.)

1275 Guido Novello (*i.e.* Guy, the younger) da Polenta, son of Ostasio da Polenta, and father of Francesca da Rimini, becomes lord of Ravenna. (See *Inf.* xxvii. 41.)

He appears to have died before 1300 and to have been succeeded by Lamberto his son, who in turn was followed (1316) by his son also known as Guido Novello da Polenta, the patron of Dante.

c. **1275** Birth of Giovanni Villani. (See under 1300.)
Death of Dante's father.
First recorded meeting of the Landsgemeinde or assembly of Uri.

1276 JAN. 11. Death of Pope Gregory X.

He is not alluded to by name in the *Commedia*; but see under 1280.

FEB. 23—JUNE 22. Pope Innocent V. (See preceding note.)

JULY 12—AUG. 17. Pope Hadrian V. (Ottobuono de' Fieschi of Genoa). *Purg.* xix. 103 *sqq.*

'One month and little more I proved how the great mantle weighs on him who guards it from the mire.' See the whole passage.

SEP. 23. Pope John XXI. (Petrus Hispanus) elected at Viterbo. (See under 1277.)

6

A DANTE CHRONOLOGY

Death of Guido Guinicelli.

Dante frequently alludes in his prose writings to this poet and in *Purg.* xxvi. 92, 97 speaks of him as 'the best father of me and others mine who ever used sweet and graceful rimes of love'. Compare *Purg.* xi. 97.

Death of Pierre de la Brosse (Pier dalla Broccia): *Purg.* vi. 22.

MAY 16. Death of Pope John XXI. '

Par. xii. 135 : 'who on earth shines through twelve treatises ' (on logic). The old mnemonic *Barbara, Celarent,* etc. of the logical manuals are attributed to him. He, alone, of all the popes contemporary with Dante, was seen by him in Paradise.

NOV. 25. Nicholas III. is elected pope at Viterbo (see under 1280).

Formation of Dollart Zee by irruption of North Sea.

Building of Campo Santo at Pisa begun, Giov. Pisano being architect (Vasari, i. 309).

Death of Niccola Pisano.

Roger Bacon condemned by a council of his order (Franciscans) in Paris, and thrown into prison.

OCT. 18. Foundation stone of (Dominican) church of Santa Maria Novella, Florence, laid, Fra Sisto and Fra Ristoro being the architects (Vasari, i. 248, 356).

Accession of Dionysius (Dinis), surnamed Agricola, Labrador, or The Husbandman, of Portugal.

Par. xix. 139. He died in 1325. The judgment of history has been more favourable on the whole than that of Dante.

Conquest of China by Mongols (Kublai Khan) completed.

John of Procida carries on his secret negotiations against Charles of Sicily, and about this time conveys to the pope from the emperor Palaeologus the 'ill-got' money which 'made him bold against Charles' (*Inf.* xix. 98-9).

AUG. 22. Death of Pope Nicholas III.

Inf. xix. 71, *sqq.* 'Beneath my head are dragged the others who preceded me in simony.' Of the eight popes who immediately preceded Nicholas III., Philalethes conjectures that the first four, Innocent IV.

1277

1278

1279

1280

(1243-54), Alexander IV. (1254-61), Urban IV. (1261-65), and Clement IV. (1265-68) are conceived by Dante to have incurred everlasting condemnation for the sin of simony. Of the next two—Gregory X. (1272-76) and Innocent V. (1276)—nothing is said ; the remaining two—Hadrian V. (1276) and John XXI. (1276-77)—we already know about.

NOV. 14. Death of Albertus Magnus at Cologne.

In *Par.* x. 98 he is pointed out by Thomas Aquinas as his ' brother (Dominican) and master '. He is frequently referred to in the prose writings of Dante.

1281   FEB. 22. Martin IV. chosen pope at Viterbo. (See below, under 1285.)

Adam of Brescia burnt for coining, at Consuma, between Val di Sieve and the upper valley of the Arno (*Inf.* xxx. 61, 104).

For date see Witte, *D. F.* ii. 216, 226.

This year is the latest assignable date for the death of Sordello. (See *Purg.* vi. 71.)

1282   MARCH 31. Sicilian vespers : End of Angevine rule in the island of Sicily.

Par. viii. 73 : ' evil rule, which ever wrath doth twine round subjects' hearts '.

Institution of priori in Florence : democratic reform.
Conquest and settlement of Wales by Edward I.
Formation of Zuyder Zee by irruption of North Sea.

1283   Beatrice first speaks to Dante.

' After the lapse of so many days that nine years exactly were completed since the above-written appearance of this most gracious being, on the last of these days it happened that . . . passing through a street, she turned her eyes thither where I stood sorely abashed, and, by her unspeakable courtesy, which is now finding its meet reward in the life everlasting, she saluted me with so virtuous a bearing, that I seemed then and there to behold the very limits of blessedness. The hour of her most sweet salutation was exactly the ninth of that day [3 P.M.]; and because it was the first time that any words from her reached mine ears, I came into such sweetness that I parted thence as one intoxicated. And betaking me to the loneliness of mine own room, I fell to thinking of this most courteous lady, thinking of whom I was

8

overtaken by a pleasant slumber, wherein a marvellous vision was presented to me' (*V. N.* 3).

This vision he embodied in his earliest known sonnet 'A ciascun' alma presa' ('To every heart which the sweet pain doth move': Rossetti), which he sent to various famous 'troubadours' of the period, Guido Cavalcanti, Cino da Pistoia, and Dante da Maiano among the rest. Their answers are extant. This, by the way, Dante tells us (*V. N.* 3) was the beginning of his friendship with Guido Cavalcanti.

To the period of seven years and one month between this date and June 9th 1290 belong the twenty poetical pieces (sonnets, ballades and canzoni) contained in the first twenty-eight chapters of the *Vita Nuova.* All are worthy of careful attention, and they are easily accessible in vol. ii. of Fraticelli's edition of the *Opere Minore* ; also in English translations by D. G. Rossetti ('Dante and his circle' in vol. ii. of *Collected Works*, 1887) or by Dean Plumptre (*Dante*, vol. ii. 1887). They include the exquisite sonnets 'Tanto gentile e tanto onesta pare' and 'Vede perfettamente ogni salute' and also the canzone 'Donne ch' avete', to which Bonagiunta of Lucca, himself a poet, refers when, meeting Dante in the sixth circle of Purgatory (xxiv. 49), he asks : "But say if I see here him who drew forth the new rimes beginning 'Ladies who have intelligence of love'." If Dante had written nothing else he would have been amply entitled to first-class rank as a poet, and they are more than enough to explain and justify his claim to the simplicity, sincerity and depth, which are the notes of the true lyric poet. "And I to him: 'I am one who mark what Love inspires, and, in that fashion which he dictates within, go setting it forth.'"

Conquest of Prussia by Teutonic knights completed.

APRIL 4. Death of Alphonso X. ('The Wise') of Castile. Not alluded to by Dante. 1284

JUNE 5. Defeat and capture of Charles, son of Charles I. of Sicily, by Roger di Loria, admiral to Peter III. of Aragon.

His life was spared through the intercession of Constance, Queen of Aragon, Manfred's daughter (a gracious pleader; see *Purg.* iii. 143); his subsequent liberation (Nov. 1288) was secured by a treaty between Alphonso of Aragon and Edward I. of England. (See *Purg.* xx. 79-84, and compare under 1305.)

AUG. 6. Decisive victory of Genoese over Pisans in seafight of Meloria. Ugolino della Gherardesca was one of the three Pisan admirals.

OCT. Ugolino is elected captain-general of Pisa.

9

A DANTE CHRONOLOGY

1285 JAN. 7. Death of Charles I. of Sicily (*Purg.* vii. 113).

MARCH 28. Death of Pope Martin IV. at Perugia (*Purg.* xxiv. 21-24).

OCT. 5. Death of Philip III. ('le Hardi') of France at Perpignan(*Purg.* vii. 103, 105); Philip IV. ('le Bel') succeeds.

NOV. Death of Pedro III. of Aragon (*Purg.* vii. 112).

c. 1285 Birth of Simone di Martino (Simone Memmi) of Siena, one of the reputed authors of the frescoes in the 'Spanish Chapel', Santa Maria Novella, Florence, and known author of the frescoes in the Papal Palace, Avignon (1339).

1286 MARCH 16. Death of Alexander III. of Scotland. He is succeeded by his granddaughter, Margaret, the Maid of Norway.

Death of Ciacco (*Inf.* vi. 42).

1287 JAN. 15. Date of Folco Portinari's will, in which he bequeaths 'fifty pounds' to his 'daughter Beatrice, wife of Simone dei Bardi'.

['*Item*, Dominae Bici, filiae meae et uxori domini Simonis de Bardis reliqui libr. 50 ad floren.']

Guido delle Colonne of Messina finishes, in Latin prose, his *Historia Destructionis Trojae*, based on the earlier French (metrical) work of Benoit de Sainte-More. A probable source of some of Dante's classical allusions.

1288 JULY. Ugolino della Gherardesca with two sons and two grandsons is shut up in the 'Tower of Hunger,' Pisa (*Inf.* xxxiii.).

1289 MARCH 4. The keys of the 'Tower of Hunger' thrown into the Arno. MARCH 12. Death of Ugolino.

MAY 29. Charles II. crowned King of Naples in Rome.

JUNE 11. Dante is at the battle of Campaldino, in which the Florentines with their Guelph allies defeat the Ghibelline league of Arezzo.

Death of Buonconte. Note the vivid description in *Purg.* v. 91-129, and by all means try to see a good map.

SEP. Dante takes part in siege of Caprona, and is present at its surrender by the Pisans (*Inf.* xxi. 95).

10

To this period belongs the group of so-called 'absence' ballate and canzoni of Dante. The sonnet 'Di donne io vidi una gentile schiera' may best be referred to 1st Nov. 1289.

Murder of Francesca da Rimini by her husband Giovanni (or Gianciotto) Malatesta ('il Sciancato') da Rimini. (Or was it in 1285? They had been married for more than twelve years.)

Death of Folco Portinari : 'a man of exceeding goodness ' (*V. N.* 22).

JUNE 9. Death of Beatrice (*V. N.* 29, 30).   1290

' And because haply it might be found good that I should say somewhat concerning her departure, I will herein declare what are the reasons which make that I shall not do so.'

The first is, that the subject would be beyond the scope of the 'present argument '; the second, that his pen is insufficient to the task of writing fitly about it ; and the third, that ' were it both possible and of absolute necessity, it would still be unseemly for me to speak thereof, seeing that thereby it must behove me to speak also mine own praises'.

Of the eleven poems in the *Vita Nuova* which belong more immediately to the period of mourning for the death of Beatrice, attention may be specially called to the canzone 'Gli occhi dolenti ' (written ' when mine eyes had wept until they were so weary with weeping that I could no longer through them give ease to my sorrow '), to the sonnet 'Era venuta nella mente mia' (written on the first anniversary of her death after he had been interrupted while he was trying to draw ' the resemblance of an angel upon certain tablets '), and to the last of the series, ' Oltre la spera, che più larga gira.' This last is thus translated by Rossetti :—

> Beyond the sphere which spreads to widest space
> Now soars the sigh that my heart sends above
> A new perception born of grieving Love
> Guideth it upward the untrodden ways.
> When it hath reached unto the end, and stays,
> It sees a lady round whom splendours move
> In homage ; till by the great light thereof
> Abashed, the pilgrim spirit stands at gaze.
> It sees her such, that when it tells me this
> Which I have seen, I understand it not,
> It hath a speech so subtle and so fine.
> And yet I know its voice within my thought
> Often remembereth me of Beatrice :
> So that I understand it, ladies mine.   11

The poet's own 'division' of this sonnet is interesting and quaint. He divides it into five parts. In the first 'I tell whither my thought goeth, naming the place by the name of one of its effects'. In the second, beginning with third line, he tells wherefore his thought goes up and who it is that makes it go. In the third (beginning with fifth line) he tells what it saw—a lady honoured—and he calls his thought a 'pilgrim spirit' because it goes up spiritually, like a pilgrim absent from his own country. In the fourth (ninth line), 'I say how the spirit sees her such (that is, in such quality) that I cannot understand her'; that is to say, my thought rises into the quality of her in a degree that my intellect cannot comprehend, seeing that our intellect is, towards those blessed souls, like our eye, weak against the sun; and this the Philosopher [Aristotle] says in the second of the Metaphysics.' In the fifth (twelfth line) 'I say that although I cannot see there whither my thought carries me,—that is, to her admirable essence—I at least understand this, namely, that it is a thought of my lady, because I often hear her name therein'. And he adds 'ladies mine' (he tells us), to show that it is to ladies that he is speaking.

After writing this sonnet (he goes on to say) 'it was given to me to behold a very wonderful vision, wherein I saw things which determined me that I would say nothing further of this most blessed one, until such time as I could discourse more worthily concerning her. And to this end I labour all I can ; as she well knoweth. Wherefore if it be His pleasure, through Whom is the life of all things, that my life continue with me a few years, it is my hope that I shall yet write concerning her, what hath not before been written of any woman. After the which, may it seem good unto Him Who is the Master of Grace, that my spirit should go hence to behold the glory of its lady : to wit, of that blessed Beatrice who now gazeth continually on His countenance Who is blessed for ever. Praise be to God.'

It is, unfortunately, impossible to fix the date at which Dante wrote these glowing sentences. It must have been before 1300, the year of the death of Guido Cavalcanti 'my chief friend, for whom I write this book'. We see in them the germ, and more than the germ, of the *Commedia.*

SEP. Death of Margaret of Norway. John Baliol and Robert Bruce become competitors for crown of Scotland.

1291 MARCH 9. Birth of Francesco (Can Grande) della Scala (*Par.* xvii. 80).

MAY 18. Capture of Acre by Malek el-Ashraf, sultan of Egypt, leading to final loss of Holy Land. (See *Inf.* xxvii. 89, 90.)

12

A DANTE CHRONOLOGY

JUNE 9. Dante makes his unfinished sketch of the angel (*V. N.* 35) and writes the sonnet 'Era Venuta'.

See Rossetti (*Col. Works*, ii. p. 85):
> 'That lady of all gentle memories
> Had lighted on my soul.'

and Plumptre (*Dante* ii. p. 239):
> 'That gentle lady came upon my thought.'

JULY 15. Death of Rudolph of Hapsburg.
(*Purg.* vii. 94): 'Who had the power to heal the wounds which have slain Italy.'

AUG. 1. Men of Uri, Schwyz, and Nidwald (Unterwalden) form an 'everlasting league,'—the beginning of the Swiss Confederation.

Gian della Bella gets the 'Ordinances of Justice' passed in Florence.

Latest assignable date for death of Michael Scot (*Inf.* xx. 116). It was probably a good deal earlier.

APRIL 4. Death of Pope Nicholas IV. He is nowhere alluded to by Dante.   1292

MAY 1. Adolphus of Nassau chosen emperor.
He died in 1298. He is nowhere alluded to in the *Commedia*.

NOV. 30. John Baliol crowned at Scone.

Roger Bacon released from prison ; dies before the end of 1294.   *c.* 1292

Earliest assignable date for Dante's marriage to Gemma dei Donati.

Also for the Canzone 'Voi che, intendendo, il terzo ciel movete' commented on in Bk. ii. of the *Convito* (see Plumptre, ii. 277).

The poem itself, and Dante's elucidation, raise subtle questions as to the poet's inner history at this time,—questions far too subtle for any but the greatest masters of the human heart.

APRIL 11. Dante and Francesco Alighieri borrow 277½ golden florins of Andrea di Guido de' Ricci. (Extant document, see Witte, *D. F.* ii. 61.)   1293

DEC. 23. Dante and Francesco Alighieri borrow 480 golden florins of Giacomo Lotti de' Corbizi and Pannocchia Riccomanni. (See preceding note.)

c. 1293 Cimabue paints the Madonna now in the Rucellai chapel of Santa Maria Novella, Florence.

See Vasari's story (i. 254-5) that its first exhibition (on a visit of Charles of Anjou to Florence) so gladdened the painter's whole neighbour-hood that the district was thenceforth called Borgo Allegri (Joyful Quarter). The story is, in its details, demonstrably inaccurate, but it at least enables us to realise how high was the place assigned to noble art in the circles within which it arose.

Gian della Bella is compelled to quit Florence.

Beginning of long and fluctuating struggle for naval supremacy between the republics of Genoa and Venice.

1294 EARLY. Charles Martel, titular King of Hungary, son of Charles II. of Naples and son-in-law of Emperor Rudolph, visits Florence, remaining for twenty days.

Par. viii. 31 *sqq.* (see especially ver. 55) speaks of a friendship between Dante and Charles Martel, which is conjectured by Todeschini to have begun now, and to have ripened in the course of a visit of the poet to Naples towards the close of this year (Scartazzini on *Par.* viii. 55).

JULY 5. Election of Pope Celestine V. (Pietro Morone) at Perugia.

DEC. 13. Abdication of Celestine V.

Inf. xxvii. 105; iii. 60: Who 'held not dear' the keys, but 'from cowardice made the great refusal'.

DEC. 24. Election of Pope Boniface VIII. (Benedetto Gaetano). See under 1303.

Foundation of the Franciscan church of Santa Croce in Florence, Arnolfo di Cambio being architect. (Other authorities say 1295; see Vasari, i. 285.)

First recorded meeting of Landsgemeinde or assembly of Schwyz.

Death of Kublai Khan at Pekin.

Death of Guittone d'Arezzo.

Purg. xxvi. 124. Dante considers him to have been a much overrated poet. ' Thus did many ancients with Guittone, from voice to voice giving him only the prize, until the truth prevailed with more persons.' See, further, *Purg.* xxiv. 56, and perhaps, also, *Purg.* xi. 97.

Death of Brunetto Latini. *c.* 1294

Inf. xv. He was born about 1220, of good family, and became a distinguished Florentine citizen. After Montaperti (1260), he was an exile in France for about nine years. He became one of Dante's masters, and the poet never afterwards forgot 'the dear, kind, paternal image of him who in the world, hour by hour, taught him how man makes himself eternal' (*Inf.* xv. 83-85).

Edward I. of England follows the policy of Simon de 1295 Montfort in 1265 (see above), by summoning to parliament, besides the prelates and barons, two knights from every shire, elected by the freeholders at the shire court, and two burgesses from every city, borough, and leading town.

Return of Marco Polo to Venice. Death of Charles Martel at Naples.

'Dante d'Alighieri poeta' is enrolled in the guild of the *c.* 1295 Apothecaries and Physicians (Speziali e Medici) of Florence.

His title to the name of poet was already well earned; of his professional attainments we know nothing. There is evidence that he had read some at least of Galen and Hippocrates, whom he places among 'those who know' (*Inf.* iv. 143). The latter is 'Great Hippocrates, whom nature for her dearest creatures made' (*Purg.* xxix. 137).

JAN. 23. Bull of Pope Boniface VIII., addressed to com- 1296 mune of Florence, denouncing Gian della Bella, and forbidding any attempt to recall him.

BEFORE MARCH 25. Death of Forese Donati, Dante's friend and companion (*Purg.* xxiii. 78).

MAY 19. Death of Celestine V. (See above, 1294.)

JULY 10. Conquest of Scotland by Edward I. : surrender of Baliol.

Giotto summoned to work in the church of St. Francis at *c.* 1296 Assisi (Vasari, i. 377-9).

AUG. 11. Canonisation of Louis IX. of France. (See 1270.) 1297

SEP. 11. Wallace's victory at Stirling.

The 'Shutting of the Great Council,' by which the

government of Venice passed into the hands of a hereditary oligarchy, took place in this year.

1298   JUNE 23. Diet of Mainz. Emperor Adolphus dethroned, and Albert I. (Duke of Austria) chosen to succeed. (See under 1308.)

JUNE. Death of Jacobus de Voragine, archbishop of Genoa, author of the collection known as *Hystoria Lombardica* or *The Golden Legend*.

JULY 2. Adolphus defeated and slain by Albert at Spires.

JULY 22. Defeat of Wallace at Falkirk.

SEP. 6. Marco Polo taken prisoner by Genoese in naval battle of Curzola.

SEP. 8. First stone of church of Santa Maria del Fiore, Florence, laid in presence of the bishop and clergy, podestà, captains, priors, and other magistrates, and the whole community, Arnolfo di Cambio being architect (Vasari, i. 287). Other accounts say 1296 (Vasari, i. 291).

Giotto is in Rome, and at work on his mosaic of the Navicella, or Ship of St. Peter, still partially extant in the portico of St. Peter's (Vasari, i. 546).

1299   MAY. Dante goes on a political mission from Florence to the commune of San Gemignano.

The only mission of the kind (before his exile) for which there is clear evidence.

JUNE 27. Bull of Boniface VIII. to Edward I. of England claiming right to decide in dispute with Scotland.

JULY. Marco Polo released. During his captivity in Genoa he had dictated his immortal book of travels to his fellow-prisoner Rusticiano (or Rustighello) of Pisa.

DEC. 25. Beginning of Jubilee Year (Christmas 1299-Christmas 1300).

'The zenith of the fame and power of Boniface, perhaps of the Roman pontificate' (Milman). See *Purg.* ii. 98 (but, so far as we are aware, it was no part of the Church's doctrine that the Jubilee accelerated the admission of souls to the purgatorial state,—only that it hastened their passage through it). There is an allusion to the Jubilee in *Inf.* xviii.

16

29, which of itself almost warrants the inference that Dante visited Rome in that year.

Death of Oderisi (Oderigi) of Gubbio, the illuminator, at *c.* 1299 Rome (*Purg.* xi. 79). (See Vasari, i. 315.)

MARCH 25. Assumed date of the beginning of Dante's 1300 journey through the realms of the unseen.

'IN THE MIDDLE OF THE JOURNEY.'

ARCH 25 (Good Friday). EARLY MORN-ING. *Dante leaves the dark wood and essays to climb the sunny hill* (Inf. i. 38).

'The time was at the beginning of the morning, and the sun was mounting up with those stars which were with him when Divine Love first set those fair things in motion.'

That is to say, it was the vernal equinox, for which the date fixed by the Julian Calendar is 25th March (viii. Kal. Apr.). From very early times the accepted tradition of the Church was that God began His work of creation on this day, and that it is also the anniversary of the Incarnation and of the Crucifixion. In Florence, and perhaps in the majority of Christian States throughout the Middle Ages, the 25th of March was also reckoned as the first day of the civil year. Dante asks us further to assume that March 25, 1300, was a Friday, and that the moon was full, and Venus a morning star. Philalethes, an admirable commentator, has pointed out that these assumptions are not in accordance with fact. But neither is it a fact that Dante in the thirty-fifth year of his life passed through the centre of the earth, and emerged at the antipodes within a couple of days. He has so filled his work with vivid realistic detail, that even the most patient and loving students are sometimes tempted to forget that, after all, the *Commedia* is a work of creative imagination.

3 P.M. *Exact completion of the 1266th year from the death of Christ* (see Inf. xxi. 112, quoted below).

DUSK. *Dante and Virgil begin their solemn journey* (Inf. ii. 1).

B

'The day was departing, and the dusk air taking the animals that are on earth from their toils.'

I 300 MARCH 25-26 (Saturday). PAST MIDNIGHT. *Dante and Virgil are about to enter the fifth circle* (Inf. vii. 98).

'Already every star is falling that was ascending when we entered.'

BETWEEN 2 AND 4 A.M. *Dante and Virgil are about to go down to the seventh circle* (Inf. xi. 113).

'The fishes glide on the horizon, and all the wain lies over Caurus' (the north-west).

ABOUT 6 A.M. *The poets are about to cross from the fourth to the fifth bolgia in the eighth circle* (Inf. xx. 126).

'Cain with the thorns already holds the confine of both hemispheres, and under Seville touches the wave; and already yesternight the moon was round: well must thou remember, for she somewhat helped thee in the dark wood.' (We must try to forget that the moon was not full on March 25, 1300.)

10 A.M. EXACTLY. *At the broken sixth arch in the fifth bolgia* (Inf. xxi. 112).

'Yesterday, five hours later than this hour, a thousand two hundred and sixty-six years were fulfilled since the way here was broken' (*i.e.* by the earthquake spoken of in Matt. xxvii. 51).

ABOUT 1.30 P.M. *Gazing down into the sixth bolgia* (Inf. xxix. 10).

'The moon already is beneath our feet.'

ABOUT 6 P.M. *In Giudecca, fronting Lucifer* (Inf. xxxiv. 68).

'But night is ascending.'

MARCH 26 (Saturday). 8.30 P.M. in northern hemisphere, and 8.30 A.M. in southern hemisphere. *Dante and Virgil have passed through the earth's centre, and are now in another hemisphere* (Inf. xxxiv. 96, 118).

'And now to middle terce the sun returns.' 'Here it is morn.' [Others interpret 'middle terce' as meaning 7.30 A.M.]

MARCH 27 (Easter Sunday). DAYBREAK. *The poets emerge from depths of earth* (Inf. xxxiv. 139).

'And thence we issued forth again to see the stars.' (The re-ascent

18

IN THE MIDDLE OF THE JOURNEY

from the centre of the earth has occupied rather more than twenty hours; the descent, including delays, had taken twenty-four.)

DAYLIGHT. *On the shore of the Southern Ocean, at the foot of the Mount of Purification* (Purg. i. 13).
'A sweet hue of oriental sapphire . . . renewed delight to my eyes, soon as I issued forth from the dead air which had saddened me, both eyes and heart.'

SUNRISE. *The angelic boat comes into sight* (Purg. ii. 1, 16).
'Already had the sun come to the horizon . . . and, lo! a light (so may I again behold it !)'

BETWEEN 9 AND 10 A.M. *The first gap on the hillside reached* (Purg. iv. 15).
'Full fifty degrees had the sun mounted.'

MIDDAY. *Arrived on the first platform of Antepurgatorio* (Purg. iv. 137).
'Come now away, see how the meridian is touched by the sun.'

LATE AFTERNOON. *Dante and Virgil meet with Sordello* (Purg. vii. 43: '*But see already how the day declines*'). *He leads them apart to the Princes' Valley, 'there to await the new day'* (vii. 69). *They see and hear the souls sit singing Salve Regina* (Purg. vii. 85).
'Before the little sun that remains sets, desire not that I should lead you among them. From this ledge better will you observe the acts and countenances of each and all.'

SUNSET. *Compline hymn—Te lucis ante* (Purg. viii. 1-18).

> Now that the daylight dies away,
>   By all Thy grace and love,
> Thee, Maker of the world, we pray
>   To watch our bed above.
>
> Let dreams depart and phantoms fly,
>   The offspring of the night;
> Keep us, like shrines, beneath Thine eye,
>   Pure in our foe's despite. —*(Newman's transl.)*

Descent of night (viii. 49).

19

A DANTE CHRONOLOGY

1300   MARCH 28 (Easter Monday). DAWN. *Dante's dream of the uplifting eagle* (Purg. ix. 13).

'In the hour when the swallow begins her sad lays, near to the morning.'

ABOUT 8.10 A.M. *Dante awakes to find that he has been carried in sleep to the gate of Purgatory* (Purg. ix. 44).

'The sun was already more than two hours high. . . . "Have no fear," said my master; "thou art now come to Purgatory."'

ABOUT 11 A.M. *Emerging from the narrow steep couloir that leads up from the gate of Purgatory* (Purg. x. 14).

'The waned moon returned to her bed for her setting before that we were forth from that needle's eye.'

MIDDAY. *Preparing to quit the first circle* (Purg. xii. 81).

'Lo! how the sixth handmaid is returning from the service of the day.'

ABOUT 3 P.M. *Preparing to leave the second circle* (Purg. xv. 1).

'As much as between the end of the third hour and the beginning of the day . . . so much appeared to remain to the sun of his course toward evening.'

LATE AFTERNOON. *Emerging from the smoke cloud of the third circle* (Purg. xvii. 1-9).

'The sun was already in its setting.'

Sunset takes place immediately after the fourth circle has been reached. Virgil improves the hours of forced inactivity by a discourse concerning love excessive, love defective, and love misapplied. Then during the night (not earlier than midnight, Purg. xviii. 76 sqq.) souls in crowds are clearly heard and dimly seen as they rush quickly past, calling to mind great examples of alacrity. Towards morning Dante sleeps.

MARCH 29 (Easter Tuesday). BEFORE DAYBREAK. *Dante's dream of the Siren* (Purg. xix. 1-6).

20

IN THE MIDDLE OF THE JOURNEY

AFTER SUNRISE. *Dante awakes, and the poets make for the ascent to the fifth circle* (Purg. xix. 39).   1300

'I lifted myself up, and wholly with the high day were already filled the circles of the Sacred Mount, and we were going with the new sun on our reins.'

BETWEEN 10 AND 11 A.M. *Statius finishes his story as the three poets are drawing near to the mystic tree* (Purg. xxii. 118).

'Already four handmaids of the day (hours) were left behind, and the fifth was at the pole of the car.'

ABOUT 2 P.M. *The poets must needs hasten on to the seventh circle, for Taurus is on the meridian* (Purg. xxv. 1-3).

LATE AFTERNOON ('*the day was departing,*' Purg. xxvii. 5). *An angel appears, who bids them pass through the flames in order that they may mount up.*

SUNSET (Purg. xxvii. 61, 66, 68-69). *The three poets lay themselves down to sleep, each on a step of the upward stair.*

MARCH 30 (Wednesday). DAWN. *Dante's dream of Rachel and Leah* (Purg. xxvii. 94).

'In the hour when Cytherea (Venus) first beamed on the mount.'

IMMEDIATELY BEFORE SUNRISE. *Dante awakes* (Purg. xxvii. 109 *sqq.*).

'Already, through the brightness before the light, which arises the more grateful to pilgrims, as on their return they lodge less far away, the shadows were fleeing on all sides, and my sleep with them ; wherefore I rose up, seeing the great masters already risen.'

The last stair is climbed, and Dante finds himself in the divine forest which ' *to his eyes was tempering the new day* ' (Purg. xxviii. 3).

MIDDAY. *Beatrice has explained the apocalyptic vision, and predicted the coming restoration of the empire* (Purg. xxxiii. 104 : ' *The sun now holds the meridian circle* '). *Matilda leads Dante and Statius to drink of the water of Eunoe.*

21

A DANTE CHRONOLOGY

THE time indications of the *Paradiso* are (for sufficient reasons, artistic and other, not difficult to guess) left less distinct.

1300

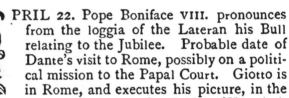

APRIL 22. Pope Boniface VIII. pronounces from the loggia of the Lateran his Bull relating to the Jubilee. Probable date of Dante's visit to Rome, possibly on a political mission to the Papal Court. Giotto is in Rome, and executes his picture, in the Lateran, of the Pope proclaiming the Jubilee (Vasari, i. 384-6). Giovanni Villani, Florentine, is in Rome.

His own words are worth quoting (*Chron.* viii. 36): 'In the year of Christ 1300 Pope Boniface VIII. made in honour of Christ's nativity a special and great indulgence. And I, finding myself in that blessed pilgrimage in the holy city of Rome, seeing her great and ancient remains, and reading the histories and great deeds of the Romans as written by Virgil, Sallust, Lucan, Livy, Valerius, Paulus Orosius, and other masters of history, who wrote the exploits and deeds, both great and small, of the Romans, and also of strangers in the whole world . . . considering that our city of Florence, the daughter and offspring of Rome, is on the increase, and destined to do great things, as Rome is in her decline, it appeared to me fitting to set down in this volume and new chronicle all the facts and beginnings of the city of Florence, in as far as it has been possible to me to collect and discover them, and to follow the doings of the Florentines at length. . . . And so in the year 1300, on my return from Rome, I began to compile this book in honour of God and of the blessed John, and in praise of our city of Florence.'

JUNE 15. Dante enters upon his two months' term of office as prior.

Practically, nothing is known of the history of his priorate, except that there were political troubles in the city, that there were banishments (actual or threatened), and that Dante and his co-priors felt it their duty to reject what they regarded as the dangerous mediation of the papal legate, the Cardinal d'Acquasparta, who accordingly withdrew in wrath after laying the city under ecclesiastical censures.

AUG. 15. Dante's term of office comes to an end.

22

A DANTE CHRONOLOGY

ABOUT DEC. Death of Guido Cavalcanti.

The story is that he had been banished, but, on account of his health, allowed to return.

Taddeo Gaddi born at Florence. Giotto is his godfather. *c.* 1300 (See 'Spanish Chapel'.)

Death of Thomas of Erceldoune (Thomas the Rhymer), pro- *c.* 1300 bable author of the Scottish metrical romance of *Sir Tristrem.*

MARCH 8. Death of Arnolfo di Cambio (born about 1301 1232). (See Vasari, ix. 247.)

APRIL. Dante is appointed to look after the widening, straightening, and repairing of the Via di San Procolo and part of the Via dell' Agnolo. For authority, see Scartazzini's *Handbook,* p. 76.

APRIL 14. Dante votes twice in the Council of the Hundred (extant document).

JUNE 18. Dante in the Council of the United Guilds votes against granting a requisition by Boniface VIII. for the loan of a hundred soldiers (extant document).

JUNE. The White party in Florence drive out the Black.

The event prophesied by Ciacco in *Inf.* vi. 64 *sqq.* Dante, speaking on March 25th, 1300, had asked that once popular Florentine: 'Tell me, if thou canst, what the citizens of the divided city shall come to?' The reply was: 'After long contention they shall come to blood, and the savage party shall expel the other with much offence. Then it behoves this [the savage party] to fall within three suns, and the other to prevail through the force of one who now keeps tacking. It shall carry its front high for a long time, keeping the other under heavy burdens, however it may weep thereat and be ashamed.'

The 'savage party' (*parte selvaggia,* or, according to another reading, *parte silvestre*) is usually understood to mean the party of the Cerchi —a leading White family, said to be indebted for the adjective here applied simply to the circumstance that it originally came from a well-wooded rural district of Tuscany—the Val di Sieve—and in fact from the parish of Acone there (see *Par.* xvi. 65). Within three suns (*i.e.* years) afterwards, in other words, before June 1304 (see 1304) a complete reversal of the situation was found to have taken place. This ultimate ascendency of the Neri or Black faction was due to the 'force of him who now [*i.e.* in March 1300] keeps tacking.' The reference may be either to Boniface VIII. or to Charles of Valois.

23

AUG. 3. Death of Alberto della Scala of Verona; he is succeeded by his eldest son Bartolommeo della Scala.

AUG. Charles of Valois, brother of Philip the Fair of France, known in Italy as Charles 'Lackland,' crosses the Alps.

Speaking on March 29th, 1300, Hugh Capet is represented in *Purg.* xx. 70 *sqq.* as saying : ' I see a time not long after this day, which draws another Charles (*i.e.* another than Charles of Anjou) forth from France, to make him and his better known. Without arms he goes forth thence, and only with the lance wherewith Judas jousted [*i.e.* sheer treachery]; and that he pushes so that he makes the paunch of Florence to burst. Therefrom not land, but sin and shame, will he gain for himself so much the more grievous as he counts light the like harm.'

EARLY IN SEPTEMBER. Charles of Valois arrives at Anagni and there holds a conference with Boniface.

SEP. 13. It stands recorded that Dante voted in the Council of the Hundred on this day.

NOV. 1. Charles of Valois enters Florence as 'Pacifier' (Paciarius) of Tuscany. (See above.)

Shortly afterwards the influence of Corso Donati, the leader of the Neri, makes itself powerfully felt. He is alluded to in *Purg.* xxiv. 82.

OCT. Beginning of struggle between Philip of France and Boniface.

The year 1301 is noteworthy, as having been in some sense the birth-year of the Ottoman Empire, in so far as in it 'Osmán (Ottoman), a Turkish chieftain, who had risen to princely rank under the last of the Seljuk Sultans of Iconium, first coined money and caused public prayer for the reigning monarch to be offered in his own name.

1302 JAN. 27. Sentence against Dante and three others (including Petracco, father of the famous Petrarch) for maladministration.

(' Fecerunt baratterias et acceperunt quod non licebat, vel aliter quam licebat per leges.')

MARCH 10. Sentence of banishment against Dante and fourteen others for contumacy.

(' Si quis predictorum ullo tempore in fortiam dioti Communis per-venerit, talis perveniens igne comburatur, sic quod moriatur.')

Dante was probably in Siena at this time, having left
Florence (see dates given above) not earlier than Sep.
13th, 1301.

As for his subsequent movements, we have a fixed point in what he
himself has said in *Par.* xvii. 70-75, where Cacciaguida, after predict-
ing his exile, says : 'Thy first refuge and resting-place shall be the
courtesy of the great Lombard.' It seems impossible to doubt that
the person here intended is Bartolommeo della Scala of Verona, who
succeeded his father Alberto on Aug. 3d, 1301, and, dying on March
7th, 1305, was succeeded by his brother Alboino, whose nobility of
character was but small, as Dante has thought proper to tell us
(*Conv.* iv. 16). Alboino in turn was succeeded in 1311 by the third
brother Francesco, better known as Can Grande, for whose eulogy see
Par. xvii. 76-92. We shall not, probably, go very far wrong if we
assume that during Bartolommeo's lifetime the poet was a good deal at
Verona. At the same time he no doubt realised, in a way that is
rather difficult for us to imagine, how much depended on his getting
back to Florence as soon as possible with all the rights of citizenship ;
his moral, political, social, and worldly status all would seem to him to
hang entirely upon this. For this end he energetically co-operated
with his fellow-exiles and political friends, and took trouble to be
present when invited to any of their deliberations. These would
naturally and most conveniently be held in Arezzo, if not in the town
at least in the territory, as adjacent to that of Florence. For Arezzo
was Ghibelline ; its podestà at this time was Uguccione della Faggiuola,
whose name for the next eighteen years is frequently mentioned in
connection with that of Dante, and the Romena of Alessandro da
Romena lay also within the territory, far up the valley of the Arno.
One important meeting in particular is mentioned as having been held
soon after the banishment (precise date unknown) at Arezzo, when it
was resolved that no effort should be spared to restore the exiled
Whites to Florence. Alessandro da Romena was chosen general-in-
chief, and Dante was named as one of twelve councillors of war.
Another place where meetings appear to have been held is the castle
of Gargonza, which lies on Aretine territory, high up among the hills
between Siena and Arezzo, about four miles from Monte San Savino

APRIL 5. His work accomplished, Charles of Valois
leaves Florence. Now, or shortly afterwards, Fulcieri da
Calboli becomes podestà of that city.

Fulcieri's cruelty to the members of the White party still remaining
in Florentine territory is alluded to by Dante in *Purg.* xiv. 58 *sqq.*,

where the poet hears Guido del Duca say to Rinier da Calboli : ' I see thy grandson, who becomes a chaser of those wolves upon the bank of the savage stream, and scares them all ; he sells their flesh while it is alive ; afterward slays them like a beast grown old ; many of life he deprives, and himself of honour. Bloody he issues from the sorry wood ; he leaves it such that, for a thousand years hence, it replants itself not in its first state'—whereat, says Dante, ' I saw the other soul grow troubled and become sad.' It is worth noticing that the ' wolves' referred to in the above passages belonged to Dante's party, and he does not seem entirely to disapprove of the expression.

The treachery of Carlino de' Pazzi, in betraying the castle of Piante-revigne in Valdarno for money, and so causing the death of many of Dante's political party, occurred in this year. See *Inf.* xxxii. 69 (Antenora). By the battle of Campo Piceno, referred to in *Inf.* xxiv. 148, is generally understood to be intended the siege and capture of the castle of Serravalle, on the frontier between Lucca and Pistoia, by Moroello Malaspina, in this year.

> JUNE 25. Boniface VIII. issues the Bull ' Unam Sanctam'.

The document ' asserts, defines, and pronounces' it to be necessary to salvation to believe that every human being is subject to the Roman Pontiff. He takes for his text the words of the disciples, ' Here are two swords,' and the Lord's reply, ' It is enough.'—Not, observes Boniface, ' It is too much.' Both are in the power of the Church. The same text is discussed by Dante in his treatise *Concerning the Empire* (*De Mon.* iii. 9), but in the opposite sense. The date of this treatise is not known, but most probably it belongs to the Luxemburg period (say about 1310 ; see below), though Witte, an important authority, has come to the conclusion that it was written before 1300. It was publicly burnt by order of the papal legate in Lombardy in 1327, and the Council of Trent placed it upon the Index of Prohibited Books.

c. 1302
> Death of Cimabue (born about 1240).
> Legendary date of story of Romeo (Montecchi) and Juliet (Cappelletti) of Verona. Comp. *Purg.* vi. 106.

It is inconceivable that the Bargello portrait of Dante should have been painted (as sometimes alleged) in this year.

1303
There is some evidence, but not of great strength, that about this period Dante was for some time at Forli, in some kind of secretarial employment, under the ' chancellor' of Scarpetta degli Ordelaffi, lord of Forli.

26

SEP. 7. Seizure and imprisonment of Boniface VIII. at Anagni (Alagna, *Anania*) by Sciarra Colonna and Guillaume de Nogaret, minister of Philip the Fair of France. He is treated with every sort of indignity, and dies a few days after his release.

Purg. xx. 86-7, Hugh Capet says: ' I see the fleur-de-lys enter into Alagna, and in His Vicar Christ Himself made captive.' Compare *Purg.* xxxii. 156 : ' That fierce paramour scourged her from the head even to the soles of her feet.'

OCT. 11. Death of Boniface VIII. : ' he of Alagna ' (*Par.* xxx. 148).

Inf. xix. 53 : Nicholas III., speaking on March 26th, 1300, in the hell of the Simoniacs, says : ' Art thou standing there already, Boniface ? By several years the writ has lied to me.' *Inf.* xxvii. 85 : Guido da Montefeltro, speaking on the same day, calls him ' the prince of the new Pharisees '. *Par.* xii. 90, in the mouth of Bonaventura, he is ' he who sits and goes astray ' ; in *Par.* ix. 132, ' no shepherd, but a wolf'.

OCT. 22. Election of Pope Benedict XI. (Nicholas Boccasini, cardinal-bishop of Ostia).

NOV. Charles of Valois (' Lackland ') returns to France. (See *Purg.* xx. 70 *sqq.*, quoted above).

MARCH 10. Niccolo Albertini da Prato, cardinal-bishop of Ostia, arrives in Florence as ' Peacemaker' (Paciarius) from Pope Benedict XI., and addresses communications to the exiles in Arezzo, calling upon them to desist from all threats and practice of war, and to intrust the peaceful settlement of their affairs to him.

1304

This was the occasion of the Epistle, usually reckoned as Dante's first, because it is supposed to have been composed by him, although it does not run in his name, but in those of 'Alexander the captain, the council, and the entire body of the White party of Florence'. It is worded with the utmost deference and respect, and promises submission to the Cardinal's demands, declaring that the writers had no other object in view than the wellbeing of their country and the peace and liberty of the Florentine people. The Cardinal's efforts proved unsuccessful, and had practically broken down entirely before May 8, at which date he went for a time to Pistoia, though he did not finally leave Florentine territory till June 4, after laying the city under interdict. In the failure of the Cardinal's pacific efforts we see the final triumph of the Florentine Neri as predicted by Ciacco in *Inf.* vi. 68, and also by Farinata degli Uberti, when, speaking on March 26, 1300, he said to Dante : ' Fifty months shall not pass ere thou shalt know how hard to practise is the art of returning from exile.' Fifty full months from March 26, 1300, bring us to May 26, 1304.

MAY. Disaster at Ponte Alla Carraja, Florence, during a dramatic representation ; many persons killed.

JUNE 10. Great fire in Florence.

JULY 7. Death of Pope Benedict XI. at Perugia.

He is not alluded to in the *Commedia,* for it is not probable that he is the DUX of *Purg.* xxxiii. 43.

JULY 20. Capture of Stirling by Edward I. Submission of Scotland.

JULY 20. Francesco Petrarca born at Arezzo.

JULY 21. Ghibellines make an abortive attempt (said to have been their second) to enter Florence by force (the affair of Lastra).

It is not likely that Dante was a member of the expedition. Petrarch's father was.

1305 MARCH. Death of Bartolommeo della Scala ; he is succeeded by his brother Alboino. (See above.)
Death of Alessandro da Romena.

Dante writes the Epistle known as his second—a letter of eulogy, condolence, and apology addressed to Alessandro's two nephews. The poet is unable to be present at the funeral—hindered neither by ingratitude nor by indifference, but by mere poverty, which prevents him from appearing with the equipage befitting a gentleman.

JUNE 5. Election of the Gascon, Bernard de Gotte, at Perugia to be Pope (Clement V.). (See below, 1314.)

The so-called ' Babylonian captivity' of the Roman Church is sometimes dated from this election, because for more than seventy years the Popes continued henceforward to be primarily French prelates and wholly under French influence. The actual transfer of the Papal See to Avignon did not take place till 1309. (See below.)

AUG. 23. Execution of Sir William Wallace in London.

28

Return of John of Monte Corvino, archbishop of Cambalu (Pekin).

Marriage of daughter of Charles II. of Naples to Azzo III. of Este. Dante calls it a disgraceful sale (*Purg.* xx. 79).

MARCH I. Expulsion of the Bolognese Whites from Bologna. Some think that Dante was among them.

MARCH 27. Bruce crowned king of Scotland at Scone.

Giotto begins work in Arena chapel, Padua.

AUG. 27. Dante is in Padua.

This assumes the genuineness of the document, vouched for by Pelli, to which he signed his name as witness ('Dante Alighieri of Florence, presently residing at Padua, in the street of San Lorenzo').

OCT. 6. Dante is in Lunigiana, and acts as procurator for Franceschino, Moroello, and Corradino Malaspina.

For the document see Plumptre, vol. i. p. lxxxv. Lunigiana is the district to the left of the traveller from Spezia to Massa on the road to Pisa. The Malaspina family were its lords. An older member of the family, Corradino, who died in 1294, is encountered by Dante in the Princes' Valley of the Antepurgatorio (March 1300). He explains exactly who he is—not the 'ancient' Conrad (two at least of that name had preceded, one in the eleventh and one towards the beginning of the thirteenth century) but a descendant of his ; his worldly-minded love to his family, he goes on to say, had caused him to neglect the interests of his own soul. Dante informs him that he had never been in Lunigiana, but that the fame of the Malaspina rang through Europe. Whereupon Conrad : 'Go now, for the sun lays not himself seven times more in Aries (*i.e.* March 27, 1307, will not have arrived) before this courteous opinion will be fastened in the midst of thy head with stronger nails than of others' speech'. (See *Purg.* viii. 109-139.)

Alagia (*Purg.* xix. 142), niece of Pope Adrian v., was wife of Moroello Malaspina.

There is some reason to imagine that Dante may have spent some time at the monastery of Santa Croce del Corvo (in Fra Ilario's home) in Val di Magra, Lunigiana. It was doubtless chiefly amid the quietness of the monastic life, and in the comparative richness of the monastic libraries of Italy, that he found means and opportunity for the profound special studies which bore fruit in the *Commedia*.

EASTERTIDE. Fra Dolcino, 'heretic,' is compelled by want of provisions and stress of wintry weather to surrender his

1306

1307

mountain fastness in the Val di Sesia, Piedmont, and is soon afterwards tortured and burnt at Vercelli (*Inf.* xxviii. 55).

JUNE. The alleged, but doubtful, date of a meeting of the Ghibelline party at the Abbey Church of San Gaudenzio in Mugello (Upper Valdisieve, Tuscany).

Dante is said to have been present, and to have signed, along with the Cerchi, Uberti, and other prominent members of the party, an agreement relating to the costs and damages likely to arise out of an attempt to get back Monte Accianico. But 1302 seems a more likely date. (See Witte, *D. F.* ii. 212, 219-220.)

JULY 7. Death of Edward I. of England. Edward II. succeeds.

Purg. vii. 131-132 was written several years after this date, and must be held to refer to Edward II. as well as to Edward I.

OCT. Persecution of Knights-Templars begun in France.

Purg. xx. 91 *sqq.* : ' I see the new Pilate . . . bear into the temple his greedy sails.'

Duns Scotus is professor of theology in Paris.

1308   MAY I. Assassination of Emperor Albert I. by his nephew John of Austria.

Elected in 1298, Albert had never come to Italy to be crowned, and Dante (*Purg.* vi. 98-105) reproaches him with this remissness, which he attributes, not wholly unjustly, to a desire for territorial aggrandisement, further referred to in *Par.* xix. 115 *sqq.* Albert is also alluded to in *Purg.* vii. 96.

SEP. 15. Death of Corso Donati.

See Forese Donati's account of it in *Purg.* xxiv. 82 *sqq.*

NOV. 25. Henry of Luxemburg chosen Emperor.

It is not unlikely that Dante may have spent a great part of this year in Paris. Some suppose him to have been in Forli. (See above, 1303.)

Death of Duns Scotus at Cologne.

c. 1308   Birth of Andrea Orcagna.

See the Campo Santo of Pisa, and the Strozzi Chapel in the transept of Santa Maria Novella, Florence.

1309   MARCH. Pope Clement V. fixes his residence at Avignon.

Beginning of 'Babylonian Captivity' of the Papacy (March 1309—Sep. 1376; see above, under 1305).

Purg. xxxii. 157-60 may be interpreted as alluding both to the trans-ference of the Papal See to Avignon and also to Dante's own residence in France.

To this period, after seven years of weary exile, with hope of return smaller than ever, may, with some probability, be assigned the Can-zone beginning 'Tre donne intorno al cor mi son venute,' and charac-terised by Fraticelli as the finest Canzone in the Italian language. Dean Plumptre, whose translation 'The three exiles' will be found in his *Dante* (ii. 297), agrees that it takes its place among the noblest of Dante's lyrics. The 'three ladies' are Justice, Generosity, and Mode-ration; they have wandered over the world as homeless, needy exiles, and now meet together round the poet's heart, and sit before the doors within which sits Love holding sovereign sway over his life. Here at any rate is a friendly house. When the poet considers this it occurs to him that his own exile may perhaps after all be an honour; if erring human judgment, or the force of destiny, will have it that the world shall treat white flowers as black, then to fall into low estate along with the good becomes praise. 'And if it were not that the beauteous image [of Florence] which has set my heart on fire, has been removed far from mine eyes, I would reckon that which is most oppressive in my lot as light. But the fire in my heart has so consumed my flesh and bones that death itself has begun to apply its key to my heart. Wherefore, even if I had been guilty in aught, years have passed since the fault was expiated, if it be true that guilt dies as soon as a man repents.'

MAY 6. Death of Charles II. of Naples. His son Robert succeeds.

AUG. 21. Henry VII. at Diet of Spires declares his inten-tion to go to Italy and receive the imperial crown at Rome.

Henry confirms the liberties of Uri, Schwyz, and Unter-walden at Constance.

OCT. Joinville finishes his *Histoire de St. Louis.*

Philip the Fair brings to public trial his charges of heresy and immorality against the deceased Pope Boniface VIII. Ultimately the prosecution is abandoned.

OCT. 24. Henry of Luxemburg crosses the Alps (reach-ing Milan on Dec. 23d).

Before this time Dante has hastened to his presence and done homage at his feet,—most likely at Lausanne (see *Ep.* vii.).

1310

NOV. 30. The Florentines resolve, in view of Henry's approach, to have new fortifications (see *Ep.* vi.).

About this time Dante writes in a tone of prophetic ecstasy 'to all and singular the kings of Italy, and the senators of the bountiful city, as well as to the dukes, marquesses, counts, and peoples,' announcing the dawn of a new and joyful day. 'Here at last is he whom Peter the vicar of God bids us honour, whom Clement, now Peter's successor, illumines with the rays of the apostolic benediction.' This Epistle may be profitably read in connection with the difficult apocalyptic vision in *Purg.* xxxii.-xxxiii.

1311 JAN. 6. Henry VII. is crowned with the iron crown of Lombardy at Milan.

MARCH 31. Dante writes a letter (*Ep.* vi.) of severe admonition to the Florentines.

It is dated 'from the Tuscan frontier at the sources of the Arno,' *i.e.* above Bibbiena, under the slopes of Falterona, perhaps at Romena. The locality is described in *Purg.* xiv. 31.

APRIL 18. Dante is still 'on the Tuscan frontier, at the source of the Arno,' whence he writes (*Ep.* vii.) to Henry, urging him to linger no longer in the north, or stay for the capture of Cremona, but to hasten southward to the main enterprise.

SEP. 2. The Florentines expressly except Dante from the amnesty they offer to their exiled citizens.

OCT. 28. Francesco (Can Grande) della Scala succeeds his brother Alboino as lord of Verona.

The help given by him to the Emperor-elect on his progress through Lombardy, 'ere that the Gascon [Clement] cheats high Henry,' is alluded to in *Par.* xvii. 82.

1312 JUNE 29. Henry is crowned emperor by the legate of Clement V. in the church of St. John Lateran in Rome.

Dean Plumptre thinks Dante may have been present, and sees a reminiscence in *Par.* xxxi. 35, and also in *Purg.* xxvii. 142.

SEP. At last (and too late) Henry enters Florentine territory.

Can Grande is made imperial vicar of Vicenza as well as of Verona.

Pretended date of forged *Chronicle* of Dino Compagni.

APRIL 25. Henry summons the princes of Italy to Pisa, 1313
and lays Robert of Naples under the ban of the Empire.

AUG. 9. Henry sets out for conquest of Naples.

AUG. 24. Death of Henry at Buonconvento near Siena.

See *Par.* xxx. 133-141 for a comprehensive view of the situation. About this time Dante probably finds a retreat in the Camaldolese monastery of Santa Croce di Fonte Avellana in Monte Catria near Gubbio. The locality is vividly described by Peter Damian in *Par.* xxi. 106 *sqq.* Mr. Butler sees a significant touch in ver. 107, ' not very distant from thy country.' This is a likely date for the fine Canzone (xxi.—Poscia ch' i' ho perduta ogni speranza ') addressed to Florence : ' Since every hope of mine hath from me gone, Thy face again, my Lady fair, to see.'

Birth of Boccaccio, at Paris or Florence (1313-1375).

Pope Celestine V. is canonised by Clement V.

Dante, however, adheres to his own view.

FEB. 17. Date of Maria Donati's will, showing her 1314
daughter, Gemma Donati, Dante's wife, to be still alive.

MARCH 30. Date of Dante's letter (*Ep.* viii.) to Guido da
Polenta, written from Venice, whither he had been sent on
a political mission.

If genuine (a considerable assumption), this document of course enables us to fix a pretty early date for the poet's connection with Ravenna.

APRIL. Uguccione della Faggiuola enters Pisa as Ghibelline leader.

APRIL 20. Death of Clement V. at Roquemaure, near
Avignon.

See the indictments in *Inf.* xix. 82-87 and *Par.* xxx. 142-148.

Between this date and July 14th, Dante writes (*Ep.* ix.) to the Italian cardinals, urging the election of an Italian pope.

JUNE 14. Uguccione della Faggiuola becomes master of
Lucca.

Dante shortly after begins to live in that city. See *Purg.* xxiv. 43.

C

JUNE 24. Bannockburn.

Distant echoes of Scottish wars in *Par.* xix. 121-123.

SEP. 17. Can Grande subdues the Paduans.

OCT. 19-20. Frederick of Austria and Louis of Bavaria chosen to the imperial dignity, each by a doubtful majority of electors. (See Milman, vii. 386.)

NOV. 29. Death of Philip the Fair.

Purg. vii. 109, 'the bane of France'; *Purg.* xx. 91, 'the new Pilate'; see also *Purg.* xxxii. 152. Dante, on March 28th, 1300, saw this king's father, Philip III., and his father-in-law, Henry III. of Navarre, in the Princes' Valley, and the knowledge of his corrupt and filthy life was a grief that pierced them. 'Philip was perhaps living when Dante wrote' (Plumptre).

Completion of the Inferno. The *Inferno* did not receive its finishing touches till after April 20, 1314, if (as is most natural) we interpret *Inf.* xix. 79 as a prophecy after the event—that Clement v.'s death would occur within nineteen years and eight months after that of Boniface. Its actual occurrence was eleven years after. Further, if the allusion to Feltro and Feltro in *Inf.* i. is to Can Grande, this would point to the conclusion that the *Inferno* was still in the making on September 17, 1314, the date of Della Scala's victory over the Paduans. At any rate, it could hardly have been written before the death of Henry. Lastly, *Inf.* xxi. 41 is generally understood as containing a reference to Lucchese affairs towards the end of 1313.

1315   AUG. 29. Uguccione della Faggiuola defeats the Florentines at Monte Catini (near Volterra).

NOV. 6. The Florentines issue a third edict of condemnation against Dante.

As his sons are included in it, it is inferred that most probably they had fought at Monte Catini in August.

NOV. 15. Victory of Swiss Confederation over Leopold of Austria at Morgarten.

1316   APRIL 10. Uguccione della Faggiuola is driven from Lucca. Both Dante and he betake themselves to Verona.

It is worth considering whether perhaps Dante's eleventh *Epistle* was not written shortly after this. It is addressed to Can Grande, and claims his friendship, but not in a manner implying that they had long been in close personal relation. As a mark of friendship the poet

34

'dedicates, inscribes, and commends to him the sublime cantique of the Comedy which is decorated with the title of Paradise'; and if the reference be to the completed *Paradiso*, then the letter must be assigned to a much later date, for the poem was certainly not finished now. But it is not impossible that the poet may in fact have sent only a specimen of the work he had accomplished, and a prospectus of the rest. The greater part of the letter consists of systematic exposition of the prologue to Canto I. of the *Paradiso* (*Par.* i. 1-38). It is painful to observe that he leaves it unfinished because 'the straitness of his personal circumstances compels him to abandon these and similar matters of service to the common weal.' But he 'has hope of Della Scala's magnificence, that at some other time the means may be placed at his disposal for proceeding with the useful exposition.' It ought not to be overlooked that he speaks of the 'executive part' of the poem in the future tense, mentioning that it 'will proceed by ascending from heaven to heaven, and that recital will be made concerning the souls of the blessed who shall have been discovered in each sphere.'

Guido Novello da Polenta succeeds Lamberto da Polenta as lord of Ravenna.

This date has special need of verification (see under 1314).

The Guelphic Florentines have now nothing to fear, and issue three successive ordinances (June 2d, Sep. 3d, and Dec. 11th) for the restoration of the rebels and exiles on certain conditions.

Giovanni Villani, 'a Guelph, but without passion,' was one of the priors of Florence in this and in the following year.

AUG. 7. John XXII. (Jacques d'Euse of Cahors) is elected at Lyons to succeed Pope Clement v.

Par. xxvii. 58-59. The apostle Peter, speaking in April 1300, says: 'Of our blood, men from Cahors (John XXII.) and Gascony (Clement v.) are making ready to drink.' This cannot have been written before August 1316, and thus we have a 'superior limit' for the date of this portion of the *Paradiso*. It is the latest occurrence in contemporary history to which Dante anywhere alludes in the *Commedia*. Possibly there is something more in the allusion to 'men from Cahors' than at first strikes the mind. Milman (vii. 339), speaking of John's promotion of cardinals, points out how clearly and deliberately it declared his sympathies, his choice being not merely confined to French or even to Gascon prelates, 'but to men connected by birth or office with his native town of Cahors. The college would be almost a Cahors in conclave.'

35

Probably therefore *Par.* xxvii. 58-59 was written considerably after 1316. The reference to Cahors in *Inf.* xi. 50 will occur to the student.

1317 Not later than January, Dante, having been urged by a friend to avail himself of the Florentine ordinances of the preceding year, writes his famous tenth *Epistle*, refusing to accept the terms of the amnesty.

In this connection may be read Dante's Canzone (xx.) 'O patria, degna di trionfal fama,' entitled by Dean Plumptre (ii. 301) 'Laudes Florentiae,' although possibly it belongs to an earlier date. Florence is addressed as 'worthy of triumphal fame, mother of high-souled sons,' who once reigned 'happy in the fair past days when each that was thine heir sought that all virtues might thy pillars be. Home of true peace and mother of all praise, thou in one faith sincere wert blest, and with the sisters four and three.' Now she is clad in mourning, full of all vice, proud, vile, enemy of peace, and those who love her most are worst regarded. Let her eclipsed faith arise once more along with justice, sword in hand, follow the lights of Justinian, wisely correct her unjust and vindictive laws, then, once more, serene and glorious, will it be hers to reign in honour; happy the soul that shall be born in Florence. 'Now, my canzone, go; bold and proud, since love doth guide thee.'

Compare the reference to Florence in *Par.* xxv. 1-12, a passage we may well imagine to have been in his mind as the anniversary of his birth and baptism returned in May of this year.

About this date, possibly, Dante finally settled in Ravenna.

Scartazzini refers, in a way fitted to stimulate interest, to a work we have not been able to see, by Cardoni (*Dante Alighieri in Ravenna*, 1864). Cardoni makes out, it seems, that the year of Giotto's coming to work in Ravenna was 1319. Now, if Vasari is to be accepted as an authority (i. 388), Giotto came at Dante's instance.

In any case there is nothing to make it likely that Dante stayed long or continuously at Verona.

DEC. 30. First Bull of John XXII. against the 'spiritual' Franciscans.

The controversy is perhaps alluded to in *Par.* xii. 120.

1318 JAN. 23. Second Bull of John XXII. against the 'spiritual' Franciscans.

Dante is at work on the *Paradiso* in Ravenna

36

DEC. 16. Can Grande della Scala is chosen captain of the **1318** Lombard league by a meeting of chiefs at Soncino.

Bruce rejects papal mediation between Edward and himself. Perhaps alluded to in *Par.* xix. 122.

Giotto, by Dante's means, is brought to Ravenna and **1319** paints frescoes around the church of the Franciscans for the lord of Polenta.

Vasari (i. 388) calls them 'ragionevole'; they have unfortunately perished.

SPRING. Robert of Naples sends fleet for relief of Genoa, besieged for some months by the Ghibellines of Lombardy. The siege continues. It is alluded to in the first Eclogue of Joannes de Virgilio. (See below.)

Dante pays a visit to Mantua and takes some part in a *c.* **1319** discussion on a question in physics.

JAN. 20 (Sunday). Dante defends his thesis *De Aqua et* **1320** *Terra* (suggested by a previous discussion at Mantua), in the 'Chapel of Santa Helena' at Verona.

This little tract might perhaps reward the attention of some student of the history of physics. There is said to be a good monograph on it by W. Schmidt (*Ueber Dante's Stellung in der Geschichte der Kosmographie*, Graz, 1876).

Exchange of Latin Eclogues between Joannes de Virgilio and Dante.

The first, by J. de Virgilio, cannot be dated earlier than the spring of 1319, for it alludes to Robert's expedition against Genoa as a possible theme for poetical treatment by Dante ; the last, Dante's reply to J. de Virgilio's second, cannot be placed later than September 1320, as we are told that it was more than a year old when found (undespatched) among his papers after his death. It has a pleasant air of cheerful detachment from the world, but is also noteworthy for its tone of wistful and tender yearning towards Florence.

Dante draws near to the end of his great work. He begins to hear and say Amen to Bernard's prayer.

Par. xxxiii. 35 : ' Preserve blameless his affections after so great a sight. Let thy protection quell human stirrings.'

Giovanni Quirino and Dante exchange sonnets.

Neither sonnet is so well known as it ought to be. Here are D. G. Rossetti's translations. Quirino writes to Dante :

'Glory to God, and to God's Mother chaste,
  Dear friend, is all the labour of thy days :
  Thou art as he who evermore uplays
That heavenly wealth which the worm cannot waste :
So shalt thou render back with interest
  The precious talent given thee by God's grace,
  While I, for my part, follow in their ways
Who by the cares of this world are possess'd.
For, as the shadow of the earth doth make
  The moon's globe dark, when so she is debarr'd
    From the bright rays which lit her in the sky,—
So now, since thou my sun didst me forsake
  (Being distant from me), I grow dull and hard,
    Even as a beast of Epicurus' sty.'

Dante replies :—

'The king by whose rich grace His servants be
  With plenty beyond measure set to dwell,
  Ordains that I my bitter wrath dispel
And lift mine eyes to the great consistory ;
Till, noting how in glorious quires agree
  The citizens of that fair citadel,
  To the Creator I His creature swell
Their song, and all their love possesses me.
So, when I contemplate the great reward
  To which our God has called the Christian seed
    I long for nothing else but only this.
And then my soul is grieved in thy regard,
  Dear friend, who reck'st not of thy nearest need,
    Renouncing for slight joys the perfect bliss.'

(See also Plumptre, ii. 307.)

AUG. 20. Defeat of Can Grande before the walls of Padua. Death of Uguccione della Faggiuola.

1321 King Robert of Naples is created by Pope John XXII. Vicar of Italy during the abeyance of the Empire.

According to Giovanni Villani, Dante was sent by Guido

Novello da Polenta on a political mission to Venice in the summer of this year.   1321

There is no evidence of any such mission in the Venetian records, or in those of Ravenna ; but this proves nothing.   For either the business was of the most trifling import, or Dante's position on the embassy must have been quite subordinate.   He was out of sight the greatest man of his century, but of absolutely no social consequence in it.   He speaks the barest matter of fact when he says, ' Truly have I been a vessel without sail and without rudder, borne to divers ports and shores and havens, by the dry wind that blows from dolorous poverty ; and have appeared vile in the eyes of many who, perhaps, through some fame of me, had imagined me in other guise ; in whose consideration not only did I in person suffer abasement, but all my work became of less account, that already done as well as that yet to do.' (*Conv.* i. 3).

SEP. 14. Death of Dante.   He is buried near the church of the Franciscans.   (See above, under 1290.)

> *Non so,* risposi lui, *quant' io mi viva :*
> *Ma già non fia 'l tornar mio tanto tosto,*
> *Ch' io non sia col voler prima alla riva.*
>
> (*Purg.* xxiv. 76-78.)

A SHORT
BIBLIOGRAPHY
OF THE
DIVINA COMMEDIA
FOR BEGINNERS

EDITIONS OF THE ORIGINAL.

HE standard modern edition of the *Commedia* is that of G. A. Scartazzini (*La Divina Commedia, riveduta nel testo e commentata*, Leipzig, 3 vols. sm. 8vo, 1874-1882; price about 30s.). Each volume can be had separately. In this edition the attempt has been made to sift and arrange all the interpretations published from the fourteenth century to the most recent times, and the result is one of great value. Of the smaller editions by Bianchi (Florence, 1 vol. 1863) and Fraticelli (Florence, 1 vol. 1864), the former is on the whole to be preferred. The remarkably cheap and good stereotype edition of Camerini, in the *Biblioteca Classica Economica* (Milan, 1 lira) gives many useful notes. The text is that of Witte, whose important ' edizione critica ' appeared at Berlin (1 vol. 4to), in 1862. The text of the *Inferno*, with a complete collation of all the MSS. at Oxford and Cambridge, is included in Dr. E. Moore's *Contribu-*

40

tions to the Textual Criticism of the Divina Commedia (Cambridge, 1889.) The Messrs. Rivington announce a new text based on the results of recent researches into the most authoritative manuscripts and editions.

TRANSLATIONS.—The best prose translation of the *Inferno* is that of J. A. Carlyle (1848, 2d ed. 1867)—'a literal prose translation, with the text of the original collated from the best editions, and explanatory notes.' In his preface Dr. Carlyle alludes to help received from 'one highly accomplished friend, whose name I am not allowed to mention.' The reader will often find himself thinking of that friend. Dr. Carlyle had intended a translation of the whole *Commedia*, but other occupations stood in the way. His work has been ably and successfully continued by Mr. A. J. Butler, in *The Purgatory of Dante Alighieri, edited with Translation and Notes* (London, 1880, 12s. 6d.), and in *The Paradise of Dante Alighieri, edited with Translation and Notes* (London, 1885). These volumes give a well-edited Italian text, with various readings, and an excellent literal prose rendering, of which free use has been made in these pages. The notes are scholarly, and of great value, especially to the student of words, who will be grateful also for the glossary at the end of each volume.

Among poetical translations, the first place, in every sense, is undoubtedly due to that of H. F. Cary (*Inferno*, 1805; *Purgatorio* and *Paradiso*, 1814), of which Lord Macaulay has said that it is 'difficult to determine whether the author deserves most praise for his intimacy with the language of Dante, or for his extraordinary mastery over his own,' while Mr. Ruskin tells us, 'if I could only read English, and had to choose, for a library narrowed by poverty, between Cary's Dante and our own original Milton, I should choose Cary without an instant's pause.'

The translation by H. W. Longfellow (*The Divine Comedy of Dante Alighieri*, London, 1867) is well known

41

A SHORT BIBLIOGRAPHY

for its close fidelity, as well as for the varied interest of its notes and illustrations.

Dean Plumptre's work (*The Commedia and Canzoniere of Dante Alighieri; a new Translation, with Notes, Essays, and Biographical Introduction* by E. H. Plumptre, D.D., Dean of Wells, London, 1886-87, 2 vols. 42s.) is by far the best contribution to the exposition of Dante yet made by any English scholar. The translation is in ten-syllabled triple rhyme, the original being eleven-syllabled terza rima.

The German student will find it well worth his while to consult the annotated metrical translation by Philalethes (John, King of Saxony), originally printed for private circulation in 1828-40, and first published in 1865-66 (*Dante Alighieri's Göttliche Comödie*, Leipzig, 3 vols., 2d edition 1871). The maps, plans, and drawings are a special feature.

ANALYSES AND COMMENTARIES.—R. E. Selfe, *How Dante climbed the Mountain* (London, 1887, 2s.). An excellent Dante primer, with special reference, as the title implies, to the *Purgatorio*.

M. F. Rossetti, *A Shadow of Dante* (London, 1884, 10s. 6d.). A very successful 'essay towards studying himself, his world, and his pilgrimage.'

F. Hettinger, *Dante's Divina Commedia: its Scope and Value*, translated from the German by Father H. S. Bowden, of the Oratory, with a commendatory letter by Cardinal Manning (London, 1887, 10s. 6d.). The chapters on the theology and ecclesiastical politics of Dante have special interest, as setting forth with some authority the modern Catholic view on the subjects to which they relate.

A convenient example of the older style of Commentary will be found in *Readings on the Purgatorio of Dante, chiefly based on the Commentary of Benvenuto da Imola*, by the Hon. William Warren Vernon, M.A. (London, 1889, 2 vols. 18s.). Benvenuto's original commentary,

42

dating from about 1379, was published for the first time at Florence in 1887 (5 vols. large 8vo).

OTHER HELPS.—Dante is his own best interpreter, and everything that he wrote has some light to throw upon his supreme work, the *Commedia*. The *Opere Minore* are easily accessible in Fraticelli's edition (Florence, 1861-62, 3 vols.—vol. i. containing the *Canzoniere*; vol. ii. the *Vita Nuova, De Vulgari Eloquio, De Monarchia,* and *De Aqua et Terra*; and vol. iii. the *Convito* and *Epistole*). Most of these have been well translated—the *Canzoniere* by Dean Plumptre (see above), the *Vita Nuova* by D. G. Rossetti (1861) and Sir Theodore Martin (1862), the *De Monarchia* ('Concerning the Empire') by F. J. Church (1879), and, perhaps the most important of all, the *Convito* (*The Banquet of Dante Alighieri,* by Katharine Hilliard ; London, 1889, 10s. 6d.).

The fullest account of the life of Dante, in English, is that given by Dean Plumptre in the work already mentioned. It was preceded by Fraticelli (*Storia della vita di Dante Alighieri,* Florence, 1861), Wegele (*Dante Alighieri's Leben u. Werke,* 1865), and Scartazzini (*Dante Alighieri ; seine Zeit, sein Leben u. seine Werke,* 1869, 2d ed. 1879). Scartazzini has also written a *Handbook to Dante,* consisting of a compendious introduction to the life and works of the poet, with references under every section to the best sources of further information, which has recently been translated, with additional notes, by Mr. Thomas Davidson (Boston, 1887, 4s.).

K. Witte's *Dante-Forschungen* (Heilbronn, 2 vols. 1879), and the *Jahrbücher,* or Year-books, of the German Dante Society, contain an immense body of valuable information and discussion on almost everything relating to Dante.

Of essays on Dante the most recent are the most thorough in workmanship and the richest in suggestion. Those of Dean Plumptre are included in the two volumes cited above. Dean Church's essay, originally published in 1850, and since reprinted in vol. ii. of his Collected Works (London, 1888, 5s.), has been truly characterised by Dean Plumptre as having marked 'the beginning of a new era in the study of the *Commedia*.' The same authority says of Lowell's essay, included in the second series of *Among My Books* (London, 1885, 7s. 6d.): 'It seems no exaggeration to say that it is simply the most complete representation of what Dante wrote, of what the man himself was, that exists in any literature.'

The *Introduction to the Study of Dante* by J. A. Symonds, an excellent book by one of the most learned and accomplished students of Italian literature and history now living, originally published in 1872, has been for some years out of print. A second edition is now passing through the press, and will be issued by Messrs. A. and C. Black early in 1890.

The earlier studies on Dante by Coleridge (*Lectures*, 1818), Macaulay (in *Essay on Milton*, 1825), and Carlyle (Lecture on *Hero as Poet*, 1840) are full of the genius of their respective authors, and mark the beginnings of a revival of an appreciative study of Dante in England, but are based on a rather imperfect acquaintance with the *Commedia* as a whole, and cannot now be accepted as adequate.

Of attempts to illustrate diagrammatically Dante's conceptions of the topography and structure of Hell and Purgatory, the best are those of Philalethes (see above) and of Michelangelo Caetani, Duke of Sermoneta (*La Materia della Divina Commedia di Dante Alighieri, dichiarata in sei Tavole*, Rome, 1865, fol.; 3d Florentine edition, 24mo, 1886, 1s. 3d.).

DANTE'S LIBRARY
an alphabetical
CATALOGUE OF AUTHORS
whom he is known to have used, or who
may be presumed to have been more
or less familiar to him.

O reader can fail to observe that
Dante was a very learned man.
Sometimes, indeed, we are apt
to overrate his erudition ; for
many points of history, science,
and philosophy in his works
that now cost us much trouble
and research to clear up were
really commonplaces in his day ;
but our tendency is more often
in the other direction—to forget how much of what
has now become, more or less, the possession of every
one (partly through his influence), was in his day very
difficult of access, or only slowly and dimly coming
within the range of human knowledge.

The student who wishes to form a fair conception
of the really large and high ideal of human learning
that prevailed in Dante's day—or, rather, which
Dante helped to form—will do well to see (or consult

in photograph) Simone Memmi's fresco on the west
side of the Spanish Chapel at Sta. Maria Novella in
Florence, and to take along with him Mr. Ruskin's
admirable exposition (*Mornings in Florence*, pp. 116-
152). The painting indeed was executed some fifty
years after Dante's death, but for practical purposes
it may be regarded as contemporary. It is intended
by the artist, Mr. Ruskin points out, to represent the
teaching power of the Spirit of God, as the companion
fresco on the opposite wall was intended to represent
the saving power of the Christ of God, in the world,
according to the understanding of Florence in that
time. In the highest point of the arch are the three
evangelical virtues : 'without these you can have no
science ; without Love, Faith, Hope, no intelligence.'
Under these hover the four cardinal virtues—Temper-
ance, Prudence, Justice and Fortitude. Beneath are
ranged the great Prophets and Apostles ; and lastly
'under the line of prophets, as powers summoned by
their voices, are the mythic figures of the seven theological or spiritual and the seven *ge*ological or natural
sciences ; and, under the feet of each of them, the
figure of its Captain-teacher to the world.' Of the
fourteen sciences enumerated seven belong to the
liberal arts,—the first three representing the trivium,
the last four the quadrivium in the arts course ; then
come the two great departments of law ; finally the
various departments of theology. Here is the list
with the name of each 'captain-teacher' following
the science he represents : 1. Grammar (Priscian) ;
2. Rhetoric (Cicero) ; 3. Logic (Aristotle) ; 4. Music
(Tubalcain) ; 5. Astronomy (Zoroaster) ; 6. Geometry

46

(Euclid) ; 7. Arithmetic (Pythagoras) ; 8. Civil Law (Justinian) ; 9. Canon Law (Clement v.)[1] ; 10. Practical Theology (Peter Lombard) ; 11. Contemplative Theology (Dionysius the Areopagite) ; 12. Dogmatic Theology (Boetius)[2] ; 13. Mystic Theology (St. John Damascene) ; 14. Polemic Theology (St. Augustine).

A glance at this list is enough to show that there were large departments of the knowledge accessible in his day that Dante could not claim to have mastered. One limitation he shared with almost all his contemporaries : he was acquainted with no language outside the Romance circle. It may be taken as certain that he did not know more than a word or two of Hebrew, Arabic, or Greek. But his work *On the Vulgar Speech* shows that he knew Provençal and French well, as well as Italian in all its dialects, and that he could read and write Latin with ease. Another limitation arose out of his outward circumstances. Even in Florence he was straitened in means ; but the greater par of his really remarkable erudition was acquired during years of wandering and exile, when, from the nature of the case, it was impossible for him to carry books with him, and he was dependent for his reading on the resources of the palatial or monastic libraries he happened to be near, and on the goodwill of their keepers. But the limitation was no doubt also in part deliberate. Some things he consented to be ignorant of that he might know others the more thoroughly. No man so learned

---

[1] The addition of the collection of decretals called the *Clementines* (1313) practically completed the ' Body of Canon Law.'
[2] Certain theological works used to be ascribed to Boetius.

was ever less of the mere bookworm or pedant than he.

The subjoined catalogue is believed to contain the names of nearly all the authors whom Dante anywhere expressly cites or who may with some probability be presumed to have been known to him. But it also includes some names, such as, for example, those of Abelard, Alexander of Hales, William of Occam, and Duns Scotus, with regard to whom his very silence is noteworthy. The idea of making such a list was in part suggested by Dean Plumptre's remark that in the names in *Inf.* iv. 136-144, 'we may almost see a catalogue of the student's library.' It will however be seen that, viewed in this light, the enumeration in question errs considerably by excess, and still more by defect : it is pleasant to think that Dante at last found so many of his authors in heaven.

It is interesting to compare our list with such library catalogues as have come down to us from Dante's period. Several of these are reprinted in the first volume of Edwards's *Memoirs of Libraries*, where further references are given. Edwards prints in full the catalogue of the (Benedictine) Monastery of Christ Church, Canterbury, dating from the end of the 13th or beginning of the 14th century. Probably the contents of the library of the (Benedictine) Badia of Florence, which Dante as a young man must have frequented most, were not very dissimilar. Edwards also gives valuable details of many other libraries, palatial and monastic, in England, Germany, Italy, and France. A prominent feature in all of them is the large number of duplicates. In the *English Historical*

Review for January 1888 is given the recently discovered catalogue of the (Benedictine) Monastery of Reading, dating from the 13th century. It includes four Bibles, one in three volumes, and three in two volumes each, including a copy 'to be kept in the cloisters'; then follow a large number of portions of Scripture, in separate volumes, usually with glosses and commentaries, five Psalters, five copies of Paul's Epistles, five copies of the *Decreta*, four of Peter Lombard, three of Hugh of St. Victor *On the Mysteries*, eighteen volumes of various works of Augustine, and so on.

A word about one book not mentioned in our catalogue. With Scripture Dante's acquaintance was delicate and profound. Yet he was not equally at home in all parts of it. Complete copies of the Bible were ponderous and rare, and certain portions of it were seldom transcribed. Perhaps apart from other rich fragments of Scripture which are imbedded in the service-books of the Latin Church, he was most familiar with the Pauline Epistles, Isaiah, Jeremiah, and the Psalms,—especially the last, from which he so often quotes, and always in such a way as makes us feel that there is a spiritual experience of his own behind the quotation. Exquisite instances are, to select two out of many examples, the *In te Domine speravi* of *Purg.* xxx., or, in *Purg.* ii., the *In exitu Israel de Egypto*, 'with so much of that Psalm as is after written'—namely, down to the end of Ps. cxv. : 'Non mortui laudabunt Te, Domine ; neque omnes *qui descendunt in infernum. Sed nos qui vivimus* benedicimus Domino.'

In judging of Dante's method of applying Scripture,
the student must always bear in mind the doctrine of
the fourfold sense which the poet has expounded in
the *Convito* and in the Epistle to Can Grande. It
was the current doctrine of that age, and enabled
men to listen, without surprise, to the political argu-
ments based in the *De Monarchia* on the words ' Here
are two swords. . . . It is enough,' and without
offence to hear some of the most sacred Messianic
texts applied to (say) Henry of Luxemburg.   Nicolas
de Lyra (*c.* 1270-1340), the learned Franciscan, whose
influence in creating a school of natural exegesis is
recognised in the old saying, ' If Lyra had not piped,
Luther had not danced,' was still a comparatively
young and obscure teacher of theology in Paris about
the time of Dante's sojourn there.   His innovating
Postils, if they commanded any attention at all, would
still be spoken of chiefly in the language of deprecia-
tion and suspicion.   They were largely indebted to
the Jewish commentator Rashi, and, to unaccustomed
eyes, their tendency would seem to be towards a
lowering and impoverishing interpretation.   Lyra
afterwards (in 1325) became provincial of his order.

ABELARD (1079-1142), an eminent figure in the history of
mediæval thought.   He is nowhere, however, alluded to
by Dante, unless indeed he was in the poet's mind in the
passage in the *Paradiso* (xix. 40-45), where an optimistic
view which he is known to have held is refuted after the
manner of Thomas Aquinas (Hettinger, p. 244). Abelard was
twice (in 1121 and in 1140) condemned for Sabellianism,
and was regarded as dangerously rationalistic.   As his

great opponent St. Bernard has it : ' While he laboured to show Plato a Christian, he showed himself a heathen.' His *Sic et Non* ('Yes and No') was the precursor of the *Book of Sentences* of his pupil, Peter Lombard, and of all the scholastic *Sums of Theology*.

AESOP (Isopo or Esopo). His fable of the ' frog and mouse ' is alluded to in *Inf.* xxiii. 4, and ' Esopo poeta ' ' in his first fable '—that of the ' cock and the pearl '—is quoted in *Conv.* iv. 30, 5. The source of the former allusion has been discovered to be in the so-called ' Planudean ' Life of Aesop, a 13th-century MS. of which was discovered in Florence and printed in 1809. The word *Ysopet* in the Middle Ages came to be a general term applied to any collection of fables; of such collections the most important from a literary point of view is that of Marie de France, who lived in the first half of the 13th century. Her work, which was almost certainly known to Dante, consisted of one hundred and three fables; these, Mr. Saintsbury tells us, ' are exceedingly well told, with a liveliness, elegance of verse, and ingenious aptness of moral, which make Marie a worthy forerunner of La Fontaine.' *Fabule Ysopice* occurs in the catalogue of the (Benedictine) Monastery of Christ Church, Canterbury (*c.* 1300).

ALBERTUS MAGNUS, or ALBERT OF COLOGNE (1193-1280), is spoken of by Thomas Aquinas in *Par.* x. 98 as his ' brother and master.' Various physical and metaphysical treatises of his are cited by Dante in the *Convito* and in the Epistle to Can Grande.

ALBUMASSAR (805-885), Arabian astronomer, author of an Introduction to Astronomy, which had been translated into Latin, is once quoted by Dante, possibly at second hand (*Conv.* ii. 14, 11—upon Mars, vapours, and the death of kings).

ALEXANDER OF HALES, ' The Irrefragable Doctor' (*ob.* 1245), Bonaventura's master, and one of Aquinas's authors, is nowhere referred to by Dante.

ALFARABIO, or ALPHARABIUS (*ob.* 950), Arabian philosopher, is cited once by Dante (*Conv.* iii. 2, 2), almost certainly at second hand, through Albertus Magnus, who is fond of quoting him.

ALFERGANO (*i.e.* 'he of Ferghana'), Arabian astronomer. His book on the elements of Chronology and Astronomy was translated into Latin in 1142. Dante quotes him (*Conv.* ii. 14, 11), at first hand it would seem, as his authority for the diameter of Mercury.

ALGAZEL, or AL-GHAZALI (*ob.* 1111), Arabian philosopher, is twice referred to in conjunction with Avicenna by Dante (*Conv.* ii. 14, 4; iv. 21, 2). His *Destruction of the Philosophers*, directed against the 'naturalistic' views of some of his Arab contemporaries, which led them to deny such doctrines as the creation of the world, in time, out of nothing, and the resurrection of the body, was much read in the Middle Ages. Algazel is frequently quoted by Thomas Aquinas.

ALPHONSO 'THE WISE' (1221-1284), the famous king of Castile, to whom astronomers were indebted for the Alphonsine Tables, is nowhere mentioned by Dante, unless indeed he be the 'good King of Castile' referred to in *Conv.* iv. 11, 7, as distinguished for liberality.

AMBROSE, bishop of Milan (*ob.* 397), a great church father, and author of numerous works, which are well represented in monastic library catalogues. He is nowhere alluded to in the *Commedia*, for the 'advocate' of *Par.* x. 119 is certainly Orosius. The omission incidentally shows how imperfect was Dante's acquaintance with Augustine's *Confessions*. An expression in Dante's ninth Epistle (1314) implies that he thought Ambrose had been unduly overlooked; was he thinking partly of his own neglect?

ANSELM, archbishop of Canterbury (*ob.* 1109), is mentioned (*Par.* xii. 137) along with Nathan and Chrysostom in the fourth heaven, that of the sun, where the Theologians are.

DANTE'S LIBRARY

But Dante had chiefly in mind the courage with which he had rebuked his king. There is no clear evidence that the poet was directly acquainted with any of his writings. The theory of the atonement in *Par.* vii. 40-45 is not that of Anselm, though approximating to it (*Par.* vii. 82-105 ; xiii. 41).

ARISTOTLE (B.C. 384-322), 'the master of those that know' (*Inf.* iv. 131), 'the master and leader of human reason . . . most worthy of faith and obedience' (*Conv.* iv. 6, 4), 'endowed almost with divine genius' (*Conv.* iv. 6, 8), 'the master of our life' (*Conv.* iv. 23, 6), 'my instructor in morals' (*De Mon.* iii. 1), 'master of the wise' (*V. E.* ii. 10), is cited at least one hundred and twenty-five times in the prose writings of Dante. All Aristotle's works had become, after a manner, accessible in the form of Latin translations from the Arabic versions of Averroes before 1225, and the poet seems to have read them all, some of them with very great care. In his later years they impressed him with a sense of the helplessness of unaided reason 'to travel over the boundless way.' 'I speak of Aristotle, of Plato, and of many others' (*Purg.* iii. 43).

AUGUSTINE, bishop of Hippo, the great church father (*ob.* 430), is twice alluded to in the *Paradiso*—once (x. 120) in connection with the assistance he received from Orosius (see below), and again (xxxii. 35) apparently as one of the promoters of the monastic life.[1] Help is taken from his *City of God* in *De Mon.* iii. 4, and he is also cited in *Conv.* iv. 9, 3 and iv. 21, 8. His *Confessions* are referred to in *Conv.* i. 2, 6 as a justifiable case of a man's speaking about himself, but if Dante had really known them, should we not have had something about Monica in the *Paradiso*, at least a word about Ambrose there, and even some allusion perhaps to Mani and Faustus in the *Inferno*? He implies some direct acquaintance with the *De Quantitate Animi* in which the

[1] The Augustine of *Par.* xii. 130 is one of the early Franciscans.

53

author gives a scale of the spiritual gradations in the ascent to God (Ep. to Can Grande : 'let my carping critics read it !'), and his ninth Epistle (1314) incidentally shows— perhaps with some self-reproach in his later years—that he thought this church father had been unduly neglected. The name of Augustine figures largely, of course, in all the monastic library catalogues.

AVERROES (1126-1198), Arabian philosopher, 'who made the great Comment' [on Aristotle], (*Inf.* iv. 144); 'the Commentator' (*Conv.* iv. 13, 3: 'he who understands the Commentator knows that he means this'). He wrote commentaries on (at least) the *Posterior Analytics*, the *Physics*, the *De Coelo*, the *De Anima*, and the *Metaphysics* of Aristotle, all of which had become accessible in Latin versions (partly by Michael Scot) before 1250. Both as a medical student, and as a student of philosophy, Dante seems to have been much influenced by him in early manhood, but afterwards to have outgrown him. His theory of the moon's spots in *Conv.* ii. 14, 7 is that of Averroes ; he refutes it in *Par.* ii. 64 and also in *Par.* xxii. 139. On *Purg.* xxv. 63, generally referred to Averroes, see Mr. Butler's note. On the other hand, Dean Plumptre has pointed out that the classification of sin in the *Inferno* is that of Aristotle's *Nicomachean Ethics* as interpreted by Averroes. 'Averroes in medical renown always stood far inferior to Avicenna. . . . At Oxford Averroes told more as the great commentator. Roger Bacon, placing him beside Aristotle and Avicenna, recommends the study of Arabic as the only way of getting the knowledge which bad versions made almost hopeless. . . . In Duns Scotus Averroes and Aristotle are the unequalled masters of the science of proof, and he pronounces distinctly the separation between Catholic and philosophical proof, which became the watchword of Averroism.' (Prof. W. Wallace in *Encyc. Brit.* art. AVERROES.)

54

DANTE'S LIBRARY

AVICENNA (c. 980-1037), Arabian philosopher and physician. He is named in *Inf.* iv. 143 along with Hippocrates and Galen. The association shows that, if he was known at all to Dante directly, it was only through his best-known work, the *Canon of Medicine*, translated into Latin by Gerard of Cremona about 1150. Michael Scot translated his work *On Animals*. Avicenna is named repeatedly in the *Convito* (ii. 14; ii. 15; iii. 14). *Par.* ii. 91-93 is an almost verbatim quotation from his *De Coelo* (Scartazzini).

BACON, ROGER (1214-c.1294), Franciscan friar, and philosopher, one of the greatest of Dante's elder contemporaries, is nowhere named by the poet. Dean Plumptre has collected much evidence which makes it not altogether improbable that the two may have met, and has pointed out various passages in the *Commedia* where Bacon's influence may presumably be traced (*e.g. Inf.* xx. 116, 117; *Par.* ii. 49, 85; xiii. 125; xxvii. 142; xxix. 105).

BEDE (*ob.* 735), 'The Venerable,' is placed (*Par.* x. 131) in the heaven of the theologians along with Isidore of Seville and Richard of St. Victor. Why? No one needs to ask who has read Cuthbert's letter describing the saint's last day on earth. Besides his *Ecclesiastical History* Bede wrote voluminously in astronomy, chronology, etc., and his name is never absent from the library catalogues, but Dante in *Ep.* ix. (1314) complains of the neglect which he suffered. Dean Plumptre (ii. 392) quotes Bede (*H. E.* v. 12) as (contrary to the usage of his age) giving a vision of a brighter even than Dante's purgatory: 'A vast and delightful field, full of fragrant flowers, in which were innumerable assemblies of men in white.'

BERNARD (1091-1153), abbot of Clairvaux, philosopher and theologian,[1] author of the hymns 'Jesus, the very thought of Thee,' 'Jesus, Thou joy of loving hearts,' 'O Jesu,

[1] The Bernard mentioned in *Par.* xi. 79 is Bernard of Quintavalle, one of the early Franciscans, indeed the first to join the order.

55

King most wonderful,' is the holy elder 'clad like the folk in glory,' 'overspread in the eyes and cheeks with a benign joy, in gesture kind as befits a tender father' who led Dante through the highest heaven, showing him the rose of the blessed, and who

> ' Grew more beautiful from Mary's light
> As from the sun the morning star serene.'

(See *Par.* xxxi. 60, 102, 139; xxxii. 107-8; xxxiii. 49.) Dante's interest in St. Bernard was awakened at a comparatively late period of his life; but, when awakened, it was very strong. Plumptre on *Par.* xxxi. 60, says, 'we can scarcely doubt, I think, that this somewhat startling change (of companionship) was meant to represent a like change in Dante's inner life.' The same author has pointed out in various places the influence on the poet's mind of the mystical theology set forth in Bernard's eighty-five sermons on Canticles and in his book *On the Praises of the Virgin Mother.* See especially the notes on *Par.* xxv. 91, and xxxi. 112, in the latter of which is quoted a beautiful passage concerning the beatific vision : 'vita eterna, beatitudo perfecta, summa voluptas . . . Quanta claritas, quanta suavitas, quanta jucunditas !' Bernard's treatise *De Consideratione* (*i.e.* 'Concerning Contemplation') is referred to in the Epistle to Can Grande ; 'let my carping critics read it !' For some interesting pages on St. Bernard, see Vaughan's *Hours with the Mystics,* i. 141-155.

BERTRAND DE BORN (*c.* 1160-1200), of Hautefort, Guienne, statesman and troubadour, 'who the young king misled to treachery' [*i.e.* Prince Henry against his father, Henry II. of England] *Inf.* xxviii. 134. He is named with commendation for his liberality in *Conv.* iv. 11, 7, and is instanced in *Vulg. Eloq.* ii. 2, as one of the 'illustrious men' who composed poetry in the vulgar tongue.

BOETIUS (*ob.* 524), statesman and philosopher, whose *De*

Consolatione Philosophiae was paraphrased by King Alfred, is not named in the *Commedia*, but is placed in the fourth heaven among the theologians as 'the holy soul which makes clear the deceitful world to whoso hearkens well to it,'*Par.* x. 125-126. There is no evidence that Dante had read his commentaries on Porphyry, or any of his logical or rhetorical works, but he is particularly fond of citing the *De Consolatione,* with its pregnant sayings (such as 'Te cernere finis,' in Ep. to Can Grande, or 'Asinus vivit,' *Conv.* ii. 8, 2); it is not improbable that Boetius is intended in *Inf.* v. 121-3, where it is said : 'No greater pain than to recall a happy time in wretchedness ; and this thy teacher knows.' In *Conv.* ii. 16, 1 (*comp.* ii. 13, 1) Dante tells us that it was Boetius and Cicero who, by the sweetness of their speech, sent him to the love, that is, to the study, of the most noble lady, Philosophy.

BONAVENTURA, 'The Seraphic Doctor' (1221-1274). 'I am the life of Bonaventura of Bagnoregio, who in my great offices ever set last the care of the left hand' (*Par.* xii. 127). His proper name was Giovanni da Fidanza, and he owes the name by which he is now best known to a happy cure, which Francis of Assisi is said to have wrought on him in his boyhood. Bonaventura was born at Bagnoregio near Orvieto in 1221, assumed the Franciscan habit about 1243, studied in Paris under Alexander of Hales, lectured in Theology there, and in 1256 became general of his order. He was not canonised till 1482 ; but, as we read in the Roman Breviary (July 14), Thomas Aquinas had (like Dante) anticipated the judgment of the Church, saying, when he found Bonaventura writing his life of St. Francis, ' 'Tis well that saint should work for saint.' Of this life of St. Francis, the account appropriately put into the mouth of St. Thomas, in *Par.* xi. 43-139, is a close epitome. Bonaventura is happily characterised by Hettinger as 'the St. Thomas of the Mystics.' There are frequent traces of his influence in the *Commedia*; Plumptre (ii. 399) has pointed out, in particular, that the allusions to Mary in the *Purgatorio* seem to have been suggested by Bonaventura's *Speculum B. V. Mariae.*

BRUNETTO LATINI. See above (p. 15), under the year 1294. His *Trésor*, written in French, is an encyclopædic compilation of cosmological, historical, geographical, botanical, and zoological lore, followed by an annotated transcript of the *Ethics* of Aristotle, and chapters in rhetoric and politics. The *Tesoretto*, in Italian rhymed couplets, relates how on his return from Spain [he had been sent thither on a political mission to Alphonso X. of Castile] he heard in the valley of Roncesvalles the news of the defeat at Montaperti. Full of sorrowful thoughts, he lost his way in a wood, where he first encountered Nature, who taught him much about physics, cosmology, and astronomy; then he met with Virtue, who gave him the rules of conduct; next he found himself before the throne of Love. The poem, which is exceedingly prosaic, is incomplete, and leaves untold the interview with Ptolemy, astronomer and philosopher, who is next introduced.

CAESAR, JULIUS, is mentioned in *Purg.* xviii. 101, as an example of energy, and in *Par.* vi. 55-57 as ' he who by the will of Rome did bear it [the eagle], hard upon the time when heaven wholly willed to bring back the world to its tranquil order '; he is alluded to in *Inf.* xxviii. 98, as having had his hesitation to cross the Rubicon overcome by Curio, and in *Inf.* iv. 123 is characterised by his ' falcon eyes.' The works of Caesar were of common occurrence in the monastic libraries, but there is no positive evidence that Dante had read either of them. All that the poet tells us about Caesar he might easily have gathered at second hand, especially from Lucan.

CASELLA, Florentine musician, an ' affable and courtly man ' (Benv. da Imola), who landed at the foot of the Mount of

58

Purification on 27th Mar. 1300 (*Purg.* ii.), is understood to have left some written scores of his music; it is somewhere stated that his setting to music of a contemporary ballad still exists in the Vatican library.

CATO. It has been suggested (see Rossetti, *Shadow of Dante*, p. 109, and Hettinger, *Div. Com.* p. 162) that Dante in giving the extraordinary prominence he does give to Cato of Utica as the champion and 'author' of liberty may have been mixing him up with the Dionysius Cato of a much later age, who wrote a collection of moral maxims which was very extensively used as an educational work in the Middle Ages. In the (14th century) catalogue of the library of the Abbey of Rievaux, for example, there occurs a 'Liber Catonis' (see Edwards, *Libraries*, i. p. 338).

CAVALCANTI, GUIDO (*c.* 1250–1300), Italian poet. He married a daughter of Farinata degli Uberti in 1267. His name occurs in *Inf.* x. 63, and he is the Guido of Florence who is mentioned thrice over in Dante's *De Vulg. Eloq.* with praise for his Italian style. It is generally supposed that he is the better Guido referred to in *Purg.* xi. 97. Specimens of his poetry may be read in English translation in Rossetti's *Dante and his Circle*. The religious element is not wholly absent from them.

CHRYSOSTOM, JOHN (*c.* 344–407), Patriarch of Constantinople, and the most eloquent of the Greek fathers, is mentioned in *Par.* xii. 137, along with Anselm and Nathan; see above, under ANSELM. The Benedictine libraries used to have Latin translations of some at least of the works of Joannes Crisostomus, but Dante does not, so far as we know, betray acquaintance with any of them.

CICERO, M. TULLIUS, is mentioned in *Inf.* iv. 141, immediately after Orpheus and before Livy and Seneca the moralist; a conjunction that would have astonished himself still more is that in *De Vulg. Eloq.* (ii. 6), where he is associated with Orosius among others as a writer of 'altissimas

59

prosas.' Dante specially mentions having read Cicero's
work *On Friendship*, and having found it useful. He also
expressly quotes, obviously at first hand, and frequently, the
De Senectute, the *De Officiis*, the *De Finibus*, the *Paradoxes*
and the *Rhetoric*. The last-named work, Villani tells us,
used to be expounded to his pupils by Brunetto Latini.

CINO DA PISTOIA (1270-1336), Italian poet, a younger contemporary spoken of with much respect by Dante in the
treatise *De Vulgari Eloquio*. He there singles out
Cino for mention along with himself as having 'with
more sweetness and subtlety composed poetry in the vulgar
[Italian] speech' (i. 10), and again speaks of their diction
as 'so wonderful, so pure, so perfect and so polished'
(i. 17). The Epistle usually reckoned as Dante's fourth
is addressed to Cino da Pistoia; its genuineness is doubted
by some. Specimens of Cino's workmanship, done into
English, can be read in Rossetti's *Dante and his Circle*.

DAMIAN, PETER (*ob.* 1072), appears to Dante in the seventh
heaven; see his vivid description of his (Camaldolese) monastery—Sta. Croce di Fonte Avellana, where the poet, we
know, passed some time after Aug. 1313—in *Par.* xxi. 106-
121. Damian became cardinal in 1058. The 'Liber Petri
Damiani de officiis divinis per anni circulum' is mentioned
in the catalogue of Reading Abbey Library (13th century).

DANIEL, ARNAUT (*ob. c.* 1189), Provençal troubadour; 'in
verses of love and prose of romance he excelled them all,'
Purg. xxvi. 118-119. A specimen of his verse is given
in *Purg.* xxvi. 140-147. Mr. Paul Meyer speaks of him
as 'remarkable for his complicated versification, the inven-
tor of the sestina, a poetic form for which Dante and
Pétrarch express an admiration difficult to understand.'
He was the author of a poem on Lancelot and Guinevere,
which Dante no doubt had studied; it is now lost, and,
with it (Witte thinks), the key to the obscure allusion in
Par. xvi. 14, 15.

DIONYSIUS, the Areopagite, is pointed out by Thomas Aquinas to Dante in the fourth heaven as 'the light of that taper which, below in flesh, saw most inwardly the nature of angels and their office' (*Par.* x. 115), while Beatrice, in the ninth heaven, after describing the nine orders of angels, says: 'Dionysius with so great desire set himself to contemplate these orders that he named and distinguished them as I do' (*Par.* xxviii. 130). The author quoted under the name of Dionysius by mediæval writers with unbounded deference, in the belief that he was the Areopagite mentioned in Acts xvii. 34, is now known as Dionysius Pseudo-Areopagita. He wrote, towards the latter half of the fifth century, four works, *On the Heavenly Hierarchy*, *On the Ecclesiastical Hierarchy*, *On the Names of God*, and *On Mystic Theology*, all professedly addressed by 'Dionysius the elder' to 'his fellow-elder Timothy.' They are often quoted by Peter Lombard and Hugh of St. Victor, and it has been alleged by a competent authority that if the writings of Dionysius were to be lost they might all be recovered piecemeal from the various works of Aquinas. The Pseudo-Areopagite was hardly yet established in his position of authority in the time of Gregory the Great (A.D. 600), and that Pope gave a somewhat different arrangement of the nine angelic orders which Dante has followed in the *Convito* (ii. 6), but retracts on Gregory's behalf and on his own in the *Paradiso* (xxviii. 135).

DIOSCORIDES (*c.* 150 A.D.), 'the good collector of the qualities' (*Inf.* iv. 139), so described on account of his treatise on Materia Medica giving an account of all the materials then used in medicine and of their supposed 'qualities' or virtues. This was a stock book in all the mediæval libraries, and had no doubt been read by Dante in connection with his professional studies as a physician.

DOMINIC (*ob.* 1221), founder of the Dominican order. See the eulogy which Dante has put into the mouth of the

Franciscan Bonaventura (*Par.* xii. 31-105). Dominic himself, so far as we know, wrote nothing except the rule of his order and business letters; but the influence on Dante of the Dominican preaching at Sta. Maria Novella may be conjectured to have been great; that of the great Dominicans, Albertus Magnus and Thomas Aquinas, we know to have been immense. Vincent of Beauvais was also a Dominican; and it is worth remembering that Master Eckhart (1260-1329), Tauler (1300-1361), Heinrich Suso (1295-1366), and Savonarola (1452-1498), were also members of the same order.

DONATUS, AELIUS (*c.* 350 A.D.), 'that Donatus who deigned to put his hand to the prime art' (*Par.* xii. 137). He was one of Jerome's masters, and wrote a Latin grammar which was used in all mediæval schools. Plumptre suggests that his introduction at the precise point in the fourth heaven where he is brought in may partly be due to the exigencies of rhyme; but something is also to be said for the high idea of the dignity of grammar which prevailed in mediæval times. See what Ruskin has to say on this part of Memmi's picture, and on grammar as 'the art of faithfully reading what has been written for our learning, and of clearly writing what we would make immortal of our thoughts.'

DUNS SCOTUS (*c.* 1265-1308). See above (p. 2) under the year 1265. 'His system is conditioned throughout by its relation to that of Aquinas, of which it is in effect an elaborate criticism. . . . In general it may be said that Duns shows less confidence in the power of reason than Thomas. . . . His destructive criticism tended to re-introduce the dualism between faith and reason which Scholasticism had laboured through centuries to overcome, though Scotus himself, of course, had no such sceptical intention' (Prof. Seth).

EUCLID (*c.* 300 B.C.), Greek mathematician: 'Euclid the geometer, and Ptolemy' (*Inf.* iv. 142). Dante, who quotes him thrice in the *Convito*, may have had some knowledge of him through a partial translation by Boetius, containing many of his definitions, postulates, axioms, enunciations, and diagrams. The *Elements* as a whole had been translated from the Arabic versions before Dante's time, but so badly as to be hardly intelligible.

EURIPIDES (*ob.* 406 B.C.), Greek dramatist, named in *Purg.* xxii. 106, was known to Dante only by hearsay.

FOLQUET OF MARSEILLES (*ob.* 1231), Provençal troubadour : 'the most powerful thinker among the poets of the south, who, from being a troubadour, became first a monk, then an abbot, and, finally, bishop of Toulouse' (Paul Meyer). Dante places him in the third heaven, that of Venus, and makes Cunizza speak thus of his fame : 'Of this shining and precious jewel of our heaven which is near to me, a great fame has remained, and, before it die, this hundredth year has yet to grow fivefold. See if man has need to make himself excellent, so that the first life may leave a second behind' (*Par.* ix. 37-42). Dante afterwards hears Folco himself tell his own story with 'that voice which charms the heaven' (*Par.* ix. 82-142). Plumptre remarks : 'It is obvious that some portions of this history presented a parallel, more or less close, to Dante's own experience, and may have drawn out his sympathy for the strangely adventurous life.' A canzone of Folquet is cited in the *De Vulg. Eloq.* (ii. 6).

FRANCIS OF ASSISI (*ob.* 1226), founder of the Franciscan order. His eulogy, based upon Bonaventura's *Life* (see above), is put into the mouth of the Dominican Aquinas (*Par.* xi.). He is further alluded to in *Par.* xxii. 90, xxxii. 35. For his preaching and writing, see Milman, *Lat. Christ.* vi. 35-37. His name was very dear to Dante, and the poet's association with the Franciscan order was specially close.

FREDERICK II., Emperor (*ob.* 1250). Dante saw him in the sixth circle of Hell (*Inf.* x. 119) with the other followers of Epicurus 'who make the soul die with the body.' But the poet was keenly alive to the service he rendered as a patron and promoter of literature, and in some eloquent sentences in the treatise *De Vulgari Eloquio* (i. 12) has for ever recorded to the praise of Frederick and his son Manfred, how they had 'followed the things which are human, scorned the things which are brutish.' Frederick is also alluded to in *Inf.* xiii. 59 as the master, the key to whose heart was held by Pier delle Vigne, and in *Inf.* xxiii. 66 as having applied a peculiar punishment to certain criminals. *Purg.* xvi. 117 refers to his quarrel with the Lombard towns.

GALEN (130-200 A.D.), Greek physician, mentioned in *Inf.* iv. 143 after Hippocrates and Avicenna, and before Averroes. Works of his were in all the libraries, and had no doubt been professionally read by Dante. The reference to the natural, animal, and vital spirits in *V. N.* 2. is taken from Galen.

GERAULT (or GUIRAUT) DE BORNEIL (*c.* 1190), Provençal troubadour : ' "the master of the troubadours," and at any rate master in the art of the so-called " close " style, though he has also left us poems of charming simplicity ' (Paul Meyer). Dante thinks him an overpraised man ; Arnaut Daniel is, in his opinion, at the head of them all, and can afford to 'let the fools talk who believe that he of Limoges (*i.e.* Gerault) surpasses him ' (*Purg.* xxvi. 120). Gerault is several times mentioned in the *De Vulg. Eloq.*

GILBERT DE LA PORRÉE (*ob.* 1154), 'the Master of the Six Principles,' is cited by this designation in *De Mon.* i. 11. His *Six Principles* (on the last six of Aristotle's categories) became a leading manual in logic, and had no doubt been studied by Dante.

GIOVACCHINO. *See* JOACHIM.

GRATIAN (*ob. c.* 1150), compiler of the *Decretum Gratiani*, and founder of the scientific study of Canon law, is pointed

64

out to Dante in the fourth heaven by Thomas Aquinas with the words: 'That other flaming issues from the smile of Gratian, who so aided one and the other court [civil and ecclesiastical] that he gives pleasure in Paradise' (*Par.* x. 104). It does not appear that Dante had carried his studies far in this direction.

GREGORY THE GREAT (*ob.* 604) is twice alluded to in the *Commedia*, once in connection with his victorious intercession for Trajan (*Purg.* x. 75)—a story Dante probably found in the Life of Gregory by Paulus Diaconus—and again, in *Par.* xxviii. 133, as having while on earth differed from Dionysius in his scheme of the celestial hierarchy, and as having smiled at his mistake when he got to glory. Dante in his ninth Epistle (1314) classes Gregory among the unjustly neglected authors. He is by no means an uninteresting writer for those who can spare time for him, and Dante must have known at least something of his works through the readings at the monasteries at which he was doubtless often present. In the monk Ulric's book on the customs of Clugny (11th century), where he gives an account of 'the manner in which the Old and New Testaments are read both in summer and in winter,' explaining at what seasons the various portions are taken up, he says, that after Martinmas come 'the prophet Daniel and the twelve minor prophets, which would not hold out if we did not add, after the last of them, from the homilies of the blessed Pope Gregory on Ezekiel. In Advent the prophet Isaiah is appointed . . . it is sometimes read through in six common nights.'

GUIDO CAVALCANTI. *See* CAVALCANTI.

GUIDO DELLE COLONNE (*ob. c.* 1287), a poet in the Sicilian dialect, twice mentioned in the *De Vulg. Eloq.* He wrote in Latin prose a *History of the Destruction of Troy*, which must have been known to Dante.

GUINICELLI, GUIDO (*ob.* 1276), of Bologna, Italian poet, often

E

mentioned by Dante, and always with some adjective expressive of the highest admiration, 'the very great' (*De Vulg. Eloq.* i. 13), 'the noble' (*Conv.* iv. 20, 3), 'the wise man' (Sonnet x. : ' Love and the gentle heart are one same thing, Even as the wise man in his ditty saith '). Dante finds him in the seventh circle of Purgatory, and there speaks of him as 'the best father of me and others mine who ever used sweet and graceful rimes of love' (*Purg.* xxvi. 97); and when Cavalcanti asks for the reason why by speech and look he shows such affection, his reply is, ' Your sweet sayings, which, so long as modern use shall last, will still make precious their very ink' (xxvi. 112-114). He was a love poet, but with strains of a higher mood, which 'led his readers into the region of the Unseen and Eternal' (Plumptre, ii. 346-7). See Rossetti, *Dante and his Circle.*

GUITTONE D'AREZZO (*ob.* 1294), Tuscan poet. Dante considered him to have been a much overrated man (*Purg.* xxvi. 124). In the *De Vulg. Eloq.* (i. 13) he is ranked with Bonagiunta of Lucca, Gallo Pisano, Mino Mocato of Siena, and Brunetto [Latini] of Florence as belonging to a quite inferior category when compared with Guido Cavalcanti, Lapo Gianni, and Dante himself.

HIPPOCRATES (B.C. 460-357), Greek physician, mentioned in *Inf.* iv. 143 after Ptolemy and before Galen, and characterised in *Purg.* xxix. 137 as, ' Great Hippocrates, whom nature for her dearest creatures made.' His name is of frequent occurrence in the library catalogues (*Liber Pronosticorum Ypocratis, Liber Amforismorum Ypocratis,* etc., Chr. Ch. Cant.), and definite traces of acquaintance with his writings have been detected by close students of the *Commedia.* The Taddeo of Bologna (*ob.* 1303) alluded to in *Par.* xii. 83 was a special student of Hippocrates, and was sometimes spoken of as Il Hippocratista.

HOMER, 'sovran poet' (*Inf.* iv. 88), was known to Dante only by hearsay, or by stray quotations. The fragments of

66

Homeric legend found in the *Commedia* and elsewhere were derived from Latin poets and such later works as the *History* of Guido delle Colonne.

HORACE, 'the satirist' (*Inf.* iv. 89), 'our master' (*De Vulg. Eloq.* ii. 4), had no doubt been studied throughout with more or less care; the only portion of his works specifically referred to by Dante is the *Art of Poetry*, which he quotes not only in *De Vulg. Eloq.* and *Conv.* but in the *Vita Nuova*, and in the Epistle to Can Grande.

HUGH OF ST. VICTOR (*c.* 1097-1141), of the Augustinian Abbey of St. Victor near Paris, who had Bernard for his intimate friend, and Peter Lombard and Richard of St. Victor for his pupils, is placed by Dante in the fourth heaven. He was the author of numerous works, including a huge commentary on the Pseudo-Dionysius, an encyclopedic work *De Eruditione Didascalica*, an ascetic treatise *On Contempt of the World*, and a treatise on systematic theology *On the Mysteries of the Faith*. Hugh was one of the leaders of the mystical school of scholastic theology, and he attained high repute. His works found their way into all the libraries (there were at least three copies of his book, *On the Mysteries*, at Reading), and he is quoted freely and as of much authority by Thomas Aquinas. Dante in his later years seems to have made direct acquaintance with his writings, and Hugh's influence has been specially traced in such places as *Par.* iii. 64 *ff.*, vii. 25 *ff.* and xxviii. 9. In common with his friend Bernard, he gave special importance to Contemplation, The Eye of the Spirit, whereby the vision of the Divine can be attained.

INNOCENT III. (1160-1216), pope, is mentioned in a purely incidental way in *Par.* xi. 92, but Dante no doubt knew his sermons and his powerful treatise *On Contempt of the World, or, the Wretchedness of Man's Estate.*

ISIDORE OF SEVILLE (*ob.* 636) appears in the fourth heaven along with Bede and Richard of St. Victor. His book of *Etymologies*

67

or *Origins*, a kind of manual of universal knowledge, was widely read in the Early Middle Ages ; it must have been known to Dante, and obviously commanded his respect. It is a work of no originality, and no direct traces of it can be pointed out with certainty in anything the poet wrote.

JACOPO DA LENTINO (*c.* 1250), Sicilian poet, is 'the Notary' mentioned in *Purg.* xxiv. 56 by Bonagiunta of Lucca as having, along with Guittone of Arezzo and himself, come short of the 'sweet new style' which Dante had attained to. He is quoted in *De Vulg. Eloq.* i. 12, with faint praise, as an example of comparative Apulian refinement.

JEROME (*ob.* 420). The passage in Jerome, referred to in *Par.* xxix. 37, is quoted in Aquinas's *Summa* (P. i. Qu. 61, Art. 3), where Dante most probably found it. Je ome' works were everywhere, but their particular type of scholars ship seems to have had few attractions for the poet, who, on the other hand, would, doubtless, be repelled by the elements of arrogance, bitterness, and intellectual pride in the imperfect character of that truly great theologian and scholar.

JOACHIM (*c.* 1145-1202), abbot of Floris in Southern Italy, is 'the Calabrian Abbot Giovacchino, endowed with prophetic spirit.' He wrote three or four theological works, including a commentary on the Apocalypse which had immense influence on mediæval millenarianism. It gave rise to a work known as 'the Introduction to the Everlasting Gospel' (with reference to Rev. xiv. 6), which, though not composed by Joachim, reflected his spirit, and was associated with his name. It became a sort of handbook among the 'spiritual' Franciscans, but has not, except in a few fragments, survived the order for its destruction given by Pope Alexander IV. in 1255. The Gospel it proclaimed was the approaching beginning of the third and last age of the world—that of the Holy Spirit—the age of perfect freedom from the letter, and of mystic contemplation, worship, and joy, to be preceded, however, by dire judgments in which

68

Antichrist was to appear. One of the predictions attributed to Joachim was that Antichrist was to be made manifest on the throne of St. Peter in 1300 ; and some commentators suppose that Dante may have seen the fulfilment of this in the pontificate of Boniface VIII.

JUSTINIAN (483-565) has the 'twofold glory'(see *Par.* vii. 6) of having been the most famous of all the emperors of the Eastern Roman Empire, and of having called into existence the *Digest*, 'by far the most precious monument of the legal genius of the Romans, and, indeed, whether one regards the merits of its substance or the prodigious influence it has exerted and still exerts, the most remarkable law-book that the world has seen' (Bryce). It is to this last great service that Justinian himself alludes, when speaking in the second heaven, he says ' by will of the primal love Whom I feel, I drew from among the laws the superfluous and the vain.' ' It pleased God of His grace to inspire in me the lofty task, and I put myself wholly into it ' (*Par.* vi. 10. 24). The same service is referred to in *Purg.* vi. 89 (' Justinian . . . put the rein in order '). Dante seems to have read the *Digest* as an intelligent layman may, and quotes it more than once (*Conv.* iv. 19, 3 ; 15, 8 ; *De Mon.* ii. 5).

JUVENAL (*ob. c.* 130 A.D.), Roman satirist, told Virgil, when he met him, of the affection of Statius for him (*Purg.* xxii. 14). He was much read in the Middle Ages. Dante quotes his eighth satire in *Conv.* iv. 29, 4, and in *De Mon.* ii. 3, and the tenth in *Conv.* iv. 13. Compare also *Sat.* vii. 84 with *Purg.* xxi. 88.

LAPO, GIANNI, Florentine poet, contemporary of Dante. See above, under Guittone, and compare Rossetti, *Dante and his Circle.*

LIVY (59 B.C.-14 A.D.), 'the famous chronicler of the deeds of the Romans ' (*De Mon.* ii. 3), is named in *Inf.* iv. 141 between Cicero and Seneca, and is often quoted, plainly at first hand, in the *De Monarchia.* See, too, *Conv.* iii. 11

and iv. 5. In *De Vulg. Eloq.* ii. 6, he is one of those who wrote 'altissimas prosas.'

LUCAN (39-65 A.D.), 'that great poet' (*Conv.* iv. 28, 5), was a nephew of the philosopher Seneca. He was the author of several juvenile poems which have been lost. His greatest and only extant work, the *Pharsalia*, he did not live to complete. Its subject is the struggle between Caesar and Pompey, and it closes abruptly (Bk. x.) in the middle of the Alexandrian war. Lucan's sympathies are republican; 'he wrote for a political regret' (Church). In the list of poets (*Inf.* iv. 88-90) he comes fourth, being preceded by Homer, Horace, and Ovid. Throughout the Middle Ages he was one of the four 'regulati poetae' (see *De Vulg. Eloq.* ii. 6),—Statius, Ovid, and Virgil, being the others—poets, that is, whom every educated person was supposed to have read at school or college. Together with Statius he was on the whole preferred to Virgil,—a preference that hardly any one now would venture to avow. He is named in *Inf.* xxv. 94; commentators have traced to him various allusions in the *Commedia*; and he is cited frequently in Dante's prose works.

MARIE DE FRANCE. *See* AESOP.

OCCAM. *See* WILLIAM.

OROSIUS, PAULUS (*c.* 390–417 A.D.), Christian historian, is pointed out by Thomas Aquinas in the fourth heaven: 'In the other little light gleams that advocate of the Christian times, of whose Latin Augustine furnished himself' (*Par.* x. 118-9). The reference is to his *Historiae adversum Paganos*, dedicated to Augustine and written at his suggestion, with the same purpose as the *Civitas Dei*, namely, to show that the circumstances of the world had not really become worse since the introduction of Christianity. Orosius's book—the *Ormista* (*i.e.* Or[osii] M[undi] Hist[ori]a)—as it was called, was known everywhere in the Middle Ages, and a paraphrase of it by King Alfred is still extant. Dante was well acquainted with it and quotes it repeatedly. He mentions Orosius as one of those who wrote 'altissimas prosas' (*De Vulg. Eloq.* ii. 6).

OVID (43 B.C.-17 A.D.), Roman poet, mentioned in *Inf.* iv. 90 after Homer and Horace. He was one of the four 'regulati poetae' of the Middle Ages (see under Lucan). Dante, no doubt, had read all his writings, but the work he chiefly quotes is what he calls 'Ovidio maggiore' (*Conv.* iii. 3, 7), that is the *Metamorphoses*, references to which are frequent in the *Convito*. They can often be traced in the *Commedia* also ; see, for example, *Inf.* xxv. 97, and *Purg.* xxxiii. 49.

PAULUS DIACONUS (*c.* 725-*c.* 800), mediæval historian, wrote a life of Gregory the Great, from which Dante most probably derived the story referred to in *Purg.* x. 76.

PETRUS COMESTOR, or PIETRO MANGIADORE (*ob.* 1179), was a native of Troyes in France ; in 1164 he became chancellor of the University of Paris, afterwards retiring to the abbey of St. Victor, where he ended his days. His *Historia Scholastica* was in substance a paraphrase of the historical parts of Scripture, especially of the Old Testament, with occasional digressions into profane history or scholastic exegesis and metaphysics. It became very popular, and was translated into German and other languages. Dante no doubt had seen it. Petrus Comestor is named (*Par.* xii. 134) along with his companions Hugh of St. Victor and Peter of Spain (see *infra*).

PETRUS HISPANUS (1226-1277) 'who on earth shines through twelve treatises' (*Par.* xii. 134), was well known to Dante through his works on logic, to which the modern student also is indebted for the *Barbara, Celarent*, etc., of the elementary treatises. He ended his days as Pope John XXI, and is the only Pope of Dante's time who is expressly named by him as having found a place in Paradise.

PETRUS LOMBARDUS (*c.* 1100-1160), 'the Master' (*De Mon.* iii. 7), 'that Peter who, with the poor woman, offered his treasure to Holy Church,' was for many years professor of Theology in Paris, and, for a few months before his death, bishop of that city. He is spoken of as 'the Master of Sentences' from his well-known theological handbook, which primarily consisted of a collection of sentences from the fathers. It became the text-book in all the theological schools, and all the *Sums of Theology* of later and abler men followed its arrangement. It was, of course, familiar to Dante, whose allusion is to the opening sentence of Bk. I.

PIER DELLE VIGNE (*c.* 1190-1249), 'who held both keys of Frederick's heart' [*i.e.* his love and his hatred] (*Inf.* xiii. 58), was the author of various Italian poems which Dante, no doubt, had read. We still have also a Latin poem of his on the twelve months of the year, and six books of his *Letters* (in Latin), which no doubt helped to deepen and render more vivid Dante's sympathy with him in the sad lot which drove him to a suicide's death.

PLATO (B.C. 427-347), Greek philosopher, is mentioned in *Inf.* iv. 134, as, along with Socrates, before the rest, standing nearest to Aristotle. In *Purg.* iii. 43, he is named with Aristotle 'and many others' as a conclusive example of the powerlessness of the unassisted human reason 'to travel over the boundless way.' In *Par.* iv. 24, Beatrice quotes 'the opinion of Plato.' This last reference is to the *Timaeus*, which Dante knew, no doubt, through the Latin translation and commentary of Chalcidius. Dante had read enough of Aristotle, Cicero, and others, to know the greatness of his name; he often refers to him in his prose works, and in *Conv.* ii. 5, 2, characterises him as 'a most excellent man.' But the *Dialogues* as a whole were quite inaccessible to him, and he never had the means of arriving at any conception of the depth and splendour of that noblest of human intellects.

PLAUTUS (*c.* 250-184 B.C.), Roman dramatist, is one of the writers about whose lot in the unseen world Statius asks Virgil in *Purg.* xxii. 97-99. It is not impossible that

Dante may have read him. He is not conspicuous in the library catalogues.

PLINY THE ELDER (23-79 A.D.), author of the *Natural History*, is another of those who wrote 'altissimas prosas.' It is not likely that Dante knew him well. The reference to Polycletus in *Purg.* x. 32 may possibly come from Pliny.

PRISCIAN (*c.* 500 A.D.), author of *Institutiones Grammaticae*, a systematic exposition of Latin grammar which was no doubt familiar to Dante. 'It may fairly be said that from the beginning of the 6th century until recently, Priscian has reigned over Latin grammar with almost as generally recognised an authority as Justinian has over Roman Law' (H. J. Roby). 'Priscianus Magnus' was in all the libraries. Dean Plumptre has justly pointed out that, so far as known to us, there is no foundation for the charge brought against the great grammarian in *Inf.* xv. 109.

PTOLEMY (*ob. c.* 151 A.D.), Greek astronomer, geographer, and mathematician,[1] is mentioned in *Inf.* iv. 142 along with Euclid and Hippocrates. His *Almagest*, as the Arabs called his *Syntaxis*, was translated from Arabic into Latin by Gerard of Cremona about 1150. It was the source of practically all Dante's astronomical knowledge. A good analysis of it is given by Professor G. Johnston Allman in the article 'Ptolemy' in the *Ency. Brit.* The Ptolemaic system of the heavens is sketched in *Par.* ii. 112 *ff.*, and also in *Conv.* ii. 3.

RABANUS (*or rather* HRABANUS) MAURUS (776-856 A.D.), Archbishop of Mainz, is mentioned in *Par.* xii. 139 after Anselm and Donatus, and before Joachim. The collocation is a singular one. He wrote commentaries and other works chiefly of a historical and linguistic nature, which were still prized and widely known in Dante's day. The poet does not betray any special acquaintance with any of them.

---

[1] The Ptolemy of *Inf.* xxxiii. 124 is most probably to be sought in 1 *Macc.* xvi. 11-16.

DANTE'S LIBRARY

RICHARD OF ST. VICTOR (*ob. c.* 1173), a Scot by birth, was Prior of St. Victor from 1162. He is sometimes spoken of as 'the Great Contemplator' from his mystical treatise *On Contemplation* ('let my carping critics read it': Ep. to Can Grande). He was a friend of St. Bernard, to whom he dedicated some of his works. Many parallelisms between the *Contemplation* of Richard and the later portion of the *Commedia* have been traced, and one writer has thought it worth while to devote thirty pages to printing them in parallel columns (see Plumptre, ii. 58). Dante (*Par.* x. 131) places him beside Isidore and Bede.

ROMANCES. The element of romantic fiction figured largely in the reading of the Middle Ages; it was chiefly to be found in French. Dante, especially in his younger days, may be supposed to have been an eager student of it; in his work *De Vulg. Eloq.* (i. 10), he speaks of the 'langue d'oil [oui] as being able to claim as its own, 'whatsoever has been either translated or originally produced in vernacular prose, such as the books of the gestes of Trojans and Romans, the very beautiful tales of King Arthur, and very many other stories and teachings.' The tale of Troy, so far as he had not read it in the ancient Latin poets, he would find in the metrical *Roman de Troie* of Benoit de Sainte-More (*c.* 1184), reproduced in his own day in Latin prose by Guido delle Colonne (see above). Dante's story of Ulysses in *Inf.* xxvi. is a striking invention of his own. For the story of Alexander (to which he frequently refers), he drew, no doubt, on the 12th century *Geste d'Alexandre* (written in 'Alexandrines'), in which were related all the fabulous tales that had fastened themselves on the name of that hero from the days of (the pseudo-)Callisthenes (3d century, A.D.). The allusion to Alexander in *Inf.* xiv. 31 is taken from an apocryphal Epistle of Alexander to Aristotle, which we find in many of the library catalogues. With regard to Charlemagne and his peers, Dante had

74

abundant access to all the *Chansons de geste*, from the 11th century onwards; for the Arthurian legends (to which he is fond of referring), he had the Latin *Historia* of Geoffrey of Monmouth (1138-47), and the compilations of Hélie de Borron and Robert de Borron (*c.* 1200), and of Rusticien, or Rustighello, of Pisa (1270-1275). We have already seen that he probably had access also to the work of Arnaud Daniel on Lancelot and Guinevere.[1]

SCOT, MICHAEL (*ob. c.* 1291), is seen in the fourth bolgia of the eighth circle of the Inferno, where the magicians and soothsayers are (*Inf.* xx. 115-117): 'That other who is so small about the flanks was Michael Scot; and of a truth he knew the play of magic frauds.' This distinguished Scotsman did important service to his own and subsequent ages by his translations (from the Arabic versions) of several works of Aristotle. His original writings deal largely with astrology, alchemy, and the occult sciences generally. His *Physiognomia* was amazingly popular.

SENECA (*c.* 3 B.C.-65 A.D.), 'the moralist' (*Inf.* iv. 141), is mentioned along with Cicero and Livy. He is quoted more than once in the *Convito*, and his essays and letters were much read in the Middle Ages. Dante had no doubt read his tragedies; but it was merely out of deference to a false etymology that in the Epistle to Can Grande he spoke of them as being 'fetid like a goat.' The writing *On the Four Cardinal Virtues*, quoted in *Conv.* iii. 8, 5, used to be attributed to Seneca.

SIGIER OF BRABANT (*ob. c.* 1300), teacher of logic in the faculty of arts in Paris, 'who, lecturing in the "Street of Straw", deduced truths which brought him envy' (*Par.* x. 136-138). He wrote a commentary on Aristotle's *Posterior Analytics*, a work entitled *Quaestiones Logicales*, and other

[1] See what Plumptre says, in his note on *Inf.* v. 67, on the interest in the scenes of the Round Table romances shown by Italian travellers in England in the 14th century.

logical treatises. Ueberweg says he originally showed
Scotist leanings, but afterwards became a Thomist,—a
change that would endear him to Dante. What the 'in-
vidiosi veri' were is a question. Ueberweg seems to
suggest the meaning of the phrase to be that Sigier was
a capital lecturer, and the envy of other teachers. Or his
change to Thomism may have seemed invidious. Some
people appear to have suspected him of heresy. Hettinger
(p. 19) in an impossible way seeks to identify this Sigier
with Sigebert of Gembloux (1030-1112), whose chief work
was a *Chronicon*, in the course of which he had a good
deal to say for the claims of the Empire against the Church.

SIMONIDES (556-469 B.C.) is mentioned, along with other
Greek poets, by Virgil to Statius in *Purg.* xxii. 107. We
have fragments of his writings, but they were inaccessible
to Dante. An allusion to Simonides in *Conv.* iv. 13, 3 is
borrowed from Thomas Aquinas (*Cont. Gentil.*), who also
knew the great poet only by hearsay.

SOCRATES (*ob.* 399) is mentioned along with Plato in *Inf.*
iv. 134, and four times mentioned in the *Convito*, but his
personality was quite dim to Dante.

SORDELLO (*ob. c.* 1266), a distinguished writer of prose and
verse in French, Provençal, and Italian. *Purg.* vi. 74:
'O Mantuan, I am Sordello of thy land.' Dante elsewhere
(*De Vulg. Eloq.* i. 15) speaks of 'Sordello of Mantua . . .
so great a man of eloquence not only in poetry but in every
form of speech.' His history is very obscure; his relations
with Cunizza are known, and we are also informed that in
1266 he accompanied Charles of Anjou in his Sicilian
expedition as far as to Novara, where he fell ill. We have
no materials for forming a direct opinion of his literary
workmanship; on this Dante, however, may be accepted
as a safe judge. He was one of the 'slothful servants',
'the men of great chances and great failures'; commentators, however, are at a loss to explain why Dante

76

introduces him at the precise point where we meet him in the ante-purgatory. One (Tommaseo) suggests that it is because Dante himself is about to pass in review a number of princes in Italy and throughout Europe, and that a similar piece of frank and severe criticism had been uttered by Sordello in one of his Provençal poems. Dean Church's essay on Browning's *Sordello* is very valuable (in *Dante and other Essays*, 1888) ; the key to that remarkable work of the imaginative intellect he states in a word : 'the influences which acted on Dante are represented as acting on Sordello.'

STATIUS (*c.* 65-96 A.D.), 'the sweet poet' (*Conv.* iv. 25, 5) gives an account of himself in *Purg.* xxi. 82-102. He was one of the four 'regulati poetae' of the Middle Ages, and was preferred on the whole, along with Lucan, to Virgil (see under Lucan). Of his writings Dante knew at least the *Thebais* well ; but he borrows also from the *Achilleis* (*Purg.* ix. 34). Mr J. S. Reid, speaking of the Epics of Statius as belonging to the class of late ancient epics which are so 'trying to the modern reader,' adds : 'the vocabulary of Statius is conspicuously rich, and he shows audacity, often successful, in the use of metaphors. At the same time he carried certain literary tricks to an aggravated pitch, in particular the excessive use of alliteration and the misuse of mythological allusion.' An instance of Statius's manner of using metaphorical expression and mythological allusion occurs in the very first sentence of the *Thebais*: 'A Pierian ardour falls upon my mind to draw out the fraternal battles,' etc. This kind of mannerism was not without its influence on Dante.

TEBALDO (THIBAUT) (*ob.* 1253), king of Navarre, was a Provençal poet of repute, mentioned with respect more than once in *De Vulg. Eloq.* (see i. 9; ii. 5; ii. 6). His son was 'the good king Thibault,' master of Ciampolo the Barrator (*Inf.* xxii. 52).

77

TERENCE (c. 185-159 B.C.), Latin comic poet, is one of the subjects of Statius's question to Virgil (*Purg.* xxii. 97); his comedies, which were no doubt known to Dante, are instanced in the Epistle to Can Grande as typical : 'a comedy begins with a certain asperity but ends prosperously.'

THOMAS AQUINAS (1225-1274), the 'Angelic Doctor', 'our good brother' (*Conv.* iv. 30, 3), one of the glories 'of the holy flock which Dominic leads upon the way' (*Par.* x. 94). He was the son of Count Landulph, and was born at Rocca Secca near Aquino (Aquinum), in Neapolitan territory, in 1225. Sent in his fifth year to the Benedictines of Monte Cassino, he studied afterwards at Naples, assumed the Dominican habit (*Par.* x. 94-5)—to the great annoyance of his relations—in 1243, and studied under Albertus Magnus (*Par.* x. 98) in Paris, graduating as bachelor of theology in 1248. The rest of his life was spent in an almost incredible activity as teacher and preacher, author, man of affairs. In connection with the business of his order he is said to have visited London in 1263. During his last illness he busied himself in expounding the Song of Solomon. He was canonised by John XXII. in 1323.

His great work on systematic theology (*Summa Theologiae*) is very often quoted in Dante's prose works, and is the immediate source of by far the larger number of the metaphysical, ethical, and theological speculations in the *Commedia*, especially in the later portions. And it is worth noting that he has three long and interesting discourses assigned to him in the *Paradiso* (x. 82-138; xi. 19-139; xiii. 34-142). But the admiring disciple by no means surrendered his independence. To take a single example—Dante's whole conception of purgatory is quite different from that of Thomas, and the poet's ante-purgatory is entirely a creation of his own.

The short biography of St. Thomas Aquinas in the Roman Breviary (March 7) is well worth reading.

78

DANTE'S LIBRARY

VINCENT OF BEAUVAIS (*ob.* 1268), a member of the Dominican
order, published, about the year 1250, an encyclopædic work
of civil and natural history, entitled *Speculum Majus*, which
is nowhere mentioned by Dante, but had a place in all the
libraries, and must have been, occasionally at least, con-
sulted by him.

VIRGIL (70-19 B.C.), 'our greatest poet' (*Conv.* iv. 26, 4) ;
'our poet' (*De Mon.* ii. 9). See the *Inferno* and the
Purgatorio, passim, for Dante's obligations. He was one
of the four 'regulati poetae' (see under Lucan).

VORAGINE, J. DE. See above, p. 16.

WILLIAM OF OCCAM (*c.* 1270-1347), 'The Invincible Doctor,'
became provincial of the English Franciscans in 1322.
'A pupil of Scotus, he carried his master's criticism further,
and denied that any theological doctrines were rationally
demonstrable. . . . The *Centiloquium Theologicum,* which
is devoted to this negative criticism, and to showing the
irrational consequences of many of the chief doctrines of
the church, has often been cited as an example of thorough-
going scepticism under a mask of solemn irony. . . . On
the whole, there is no reason to doubt Occam's honest
adhesion to each of the two guides whose contrariety he
laboured to display' (Prof. Seth).

AN INDEX

TO THE

Dante Chronology

AND

the other Notes

F

INDEX

INDEX

83

INDEX

THE END

EDINBURGH UNIVERSITY PRESS

T. AND A. CONSTABLE

Printers to Her Majesty

MDCCCXC

CPSIA information can be obtained
at www.ICGtesting.com
Printed in the USA
BVHW03*1205090518
515746BV00012B/505/P